Praise for *Phanto*

"As Hall and Petonito reveal, when y
may not be human . . ."

— Nick Redfern, author of *The Slenderman Mysteries*

"*Phantom Messages* is the most appropriate title I could have imagined for this fascinating book. This is without doubt one of those rare books that so excite and engage from page one that you would be advised to be comfortable with coffee already poured. This fact is of itself an important one, because it highlights part of a larger and more important aspect of researching these mysterious events.

Something tries to communicate from time to time and in bizarre ways. Someone or thing is interacting with humanity in various ways and in my own research has shown itself in UFO experiences and crop circle manifestations too. Even when humans are themselves involved in deceptions, such as hoaxing, the Phantom can and does show up. *Phantom Messages* is more than a captivating read, it is an opportunity to consider a larger reality than we have acknowledged in the past. William and Jimmy are to be congratulated in producing this one-of-a-kind book which I am honored to endorse."

— Colin Andrews, author of *On the Edge of Reality*

"Mind-boggling mystery messages from the dead, spirits, entities, our future selves, and more; all guaranteed to prickle your skin and make you realize that our reality has no boundaries. Starting this book is like taking a chip out of the bag—you can't stop until you're done. A great read and a researcher's dream!"

— Rosemary Ellen Guiley, author of *Contact with the Dead*

"Thought-provoking and entertaining! Truly a holistic go-to resource filled with diverse cases of phantom messages. A must-read for anyone interested in unexplainable communications or ghostly encounters!"

— Brandon Massullo, parapsychologist and author of *The Ghost Studies*

"*Phantom Messages* is the guilty pleasure I have long awaited. It is a fantastic collection of true stories guaranteed to chill your bones and thrill you at the same time. Stories go from ghostly entities communicating unthinkable horror to pictures of deceased loved ones that talk to people who hear themselves 'die' on the phone. This is a beautifully composed symphony of horror and fright chills that harken back to the old Kolchak

The Nightstalker series on television. You will devour it in a single sit-down but try NOT to be alone at night in your home . . . lest your phone start buzzing with the CALLER UNKNOWN flashing in the darkness . . ."
—John DeSouza, author of *The Extra-Dimensionals*

"Anyone interested in the field, whether they are a beginner, intermediate, or advanced researcher or like-minded soul, will find this to be a great read with useful information."
—Alexandra Holzer, author, *Growing Up Haunted*, intuitive and physical researcher

"In the world of paranormal publishing there are few original concepts. This book, *Phantom Messages,* is thankfully one of those rare occasions. Jimmy Petonito and Bill Hall have delved into a fascinating area of after-death communication that has gone largely neglected to create a page turner of a book. If you, like me, are interested in how our loved ones reach out from beyond, you need to read *Phantom Messages* today!"
—Jim Harold, Host, Paranormal Podcast, Jim Harold's Campfire

Past Praise for the work of William J. Hall

"*The World's Most Haunted House* grabbed me from the beginning . . . it is a page turner. This work is a contribution to the nonfiction paranormal genre and one that needs to be read."
—Edwin F. Becker, author of *True Haunting*

"Bill Hall chronicles his investigation into claims of an allegedly haunted house with great enthusiasm, offering a tremendous amount of detail and evidence not found in similar works. His conscientious efforts to lay out facts, observations, and testimony in a clear, concise manner makes *The Haunted House Diaries* a compelling read for anyone who enjoys the paranormal."
—Ray Bendici, editor of *Connecticut Magazine*, author, and owner of *Damnedct.com*

"In forty-five years of paranormal research, this is the deepest and widest-ranging case I've ever tackled. It makes me wonder what I was missing in earlier cases."
—Paul F. Eno, award-winning journalist and cohost of *Behind the Paranormal with Paul & Ben Eno*

Chilling Phone Calls,
Letters, Emails, and Texts
from Unknown Realms

PHANTOM
MESSAGES

William J. Hall & Jimmy Petonito

disinformation®

This edition first published in 2018 by Disinformation Books, an imprint of
Red Wheel/Weiser, LLC
With offices at:
65 Parker Street, Suite 7
Newburyport, MA 01950
www.redwheelweiser.com

ISBN: 978-1-938875-17-5
Library of Congress Cataloging-in-Publication Data
available upon request.

Cover design by Kathryn Sky-Peck
Cover photograph © TK
Interior by Gina Schenck
Typeset in Adobe Garamond Pro and Abadi Condensed

Printed in Canada
MAR
10 9 8 7 6 5 4 3 2 1

William J. Hall
In Memory of Dad

Jimmy Petonito
Valerie, Holly, and Heidi Petonito

Acknowledgments

Special thanks to:

Rita Rosenkranz: Literary Agent

Susan Shulman: Motion Picture and Television Agent

Michael Pye: Senior Acquisitions Editor

Laurie Kelly-Pye: Sales Director

Gina Schenck: Copy Editor

Kathryn Sky-Peck: For another stellar cover design

Illustrations: Mike Mendes, Koren Harpaz, Heidi Petonito, and Holly Petonito

Photo preparation: The super sweet, beautiful, and talented Nancy Balisciano Cardone

The rest of the delightful folks at Red Wheel/Weiser.

Tony Damato for the lead on the troll encounters.

Other researchers of this phenomena, notably D. Scott Rogo, Raymond Bayless, Callum E. Cooper, and Anabela Cardoso. We thank you for igniting our passion for the subject.

Fellow investigators Rick Clark and Shane Sirois, Gary Rowe, Colin Andrews, Nick Redfern, and all who contributed to this undertaking.

All of the folks in these cases who braved the storm and told their stories anyway.

To all of our fans (you know who you are).

Bill would like to thank Jimmy, and Jimmy would like to thank Bill.

"Do not drink too deeply of the fount of knowledge lest you learn something you do not wish to know."
—J. K. Rowling

Unknown entity. *Illustration by Holly Petonito.*

Contents

SECTION 1

METHODOLOGY

Admittedly not scientists by trade, we are scientists at heart and approach. Any phenomena that violates well-established physics where we have a clear idea of what's going on requires extraordinary evidence to support its claims. And for a theory to be scientific, we must be able to tell how it can be proven false. If we refuse to alter our theories or beliefs based on new undisputable data, then we need to realize it's us who are close-minded. At the opposite end of the spectrum, you have all the evidence needed *in the blink of an eye* when it happens to you. What's behind it all is a different story, and one that we shall discuss later.

The cases contained within these pages are considered most remarkable in nature. Some debunking is included to show how care must be taken in our search. We can't obtain evidence that would meet the scientific standard used to test even ordinary phenomena. We understand. For science to be as accurate as it can be, it needs to be highly disciplined. That is why gravity is still a theory. We know gravity exists and how it works with confidence. Since we might still discover new information about this force, it is called a theory. This can be frustrating to those who have experienced the paranormal, but understand such strict designations are necessary.

Carefully consider what Dr. Asimov elegantly pointed out: "There is not a single mystical belief that is not supported by numerous cases of eyewitness evidence."

Nevertheless, this is not crowd hysteria or groupthink. Something is going on here. If a study finally revealed the key to this quest, it certainly would be stimulating. These messages occur under inexplicable circumstances and are shared by a significant number of people throughout the world. Are they all lying? Are they all crazy? Are their memories and judgements *that* off? More than half of these cases contain witnesses, which swiftly invalidates the old hallucination excuse when examined under scrutiny.

There are even cases in which dated voice mail messages are preserved. These unearthly artifacts are evidence that *someone* called. Frequency, coupled with additional paranormal phenomena, provides enhanced confidence in the validity of these messengers. By identifying data points for each case and the unique elements that help define them, we can look to discover more about the components of phantom visitors. Each case will have "characteristics," which will be summarized as follows:

Message Type: Landline, computer screen, email, text, cell phone, written letter, television set, radio, cable box, and so on.

Frequency: Once, twice, or multiple (three or more).

Other Phenomena: None, part of a larger haunting, in a flap area.

From: No one knows, but we will list proposed possibilities.

Witnesses: Others experienced it, same time or separate occurrences.

Elements: Special notes are listed here, such as noting if it's a warning call, one that holds a prediction, a time slip, or other element or take away.

It's okay to question these mysterious experiences, despite having witnesses or technical impossibilities. One thing is certain: *These messages are life changing to those who experience them.* Our hope is that this work in some ways challenges answers, heightens wonder, and fuels your quest for exploring the unexplained.

1

ENTER THE WORLD OF PHANTOM MESSAGES

If you want to find the secrets of the universe, think in
terms of energy, frequency, and vibration.
—Nikola Tesla

Alexander Bell revealed a magical mystical device that promised to send and receive conversations between people who couldn't see each other in person. Onlookers remained skeptical. Prior to Bell, uninvited Morse code messages plagued recipients with striking similarity to the messages that arrived by letter, phone, and other modern electronics.

Thomas Edison, raised by spiritualist parents, instinctively desired to construct a telephone that could make long-distance calls to the dead. Bell also harbored the identical dream of such a device. With all the wonderous technology being introduced, an otherworldly widget was the next logical breakthrough. It's not surprising that any new communication device spurs our imagination to actively consider interdimensional communication as one potential use.

As a result of this speculation, psychic telephone experiments in the 1940s were plentiful in England and America. Any strange voices received were suspected of coming from unknown realms.

Science fiction imagines what we later engineer into existence. And science fiction has a history of dramatizing phone calls initiated from beyond. In 1964, our favorite series *The Twilight Zone* aired an episode entitled "Night Call," which told an eerie story about phantom message phenomena.

The episode featured a woman who lost her fiancé in a car crash she caused. When he was alive, her fiancé always did what she wanted. Menacing phone calls began and were thought to be a cruel prank; she told the caller to leave her alone. Later, she discovered the calls were coming from the fiancé's grave. When he calls again, she begs him not to go, but he says he always did what she wanted, so he had to leave her alone.

The Final Destination movie series is a recent pop culture demonstration of phantom messaging acting as a warning of future events. In the case of these poor kids, it was the result of owing a debt caused by escaping death. In *Final Destination 5*, the bus's radio station is interrupted by the song "Dust in the Wind," cutting through the signal and ominously playing right before a bridge collapses, killing motorists on their way across.

We look to our dependable advanced communication devices and imagine them sending us a variety of messages or signs, especially from loved ones we can no longer communicate with—or can we? What about when the calls are unexpected and outside of any mourning period? What about when there are witnesses? And how about when they continue for weeks, months, or in some cases, even years?

Phantom messages are diverse. Some contacts involve unknown entities, people you know, or even extraterrestrial encounters. They can be an isolated communication or a gruesome companion to broader paranormal manifestations.

In instances where a loved one is making contact, we look to examine if they are most likely to occur within a heightened bereavement state during which vivid hallucinations are the norm versus the exception. Calls within twenty-four hours or within weeks following the death of a loved one are the most suspect. However, not all recipients know at the time of contact that the person is dead. In the collection of cases throughout the years, it appears to be a common experience that when the listener realizes the person is dead, the call ends abruptly. The line goes dead, as the pun would go. After having one of these calls, the phone company often has no record of it, even when voice mails are received as tangible lingering evidence.

Calls from the living that were never made is another part of phantom messages. In this brand of "the living haunting the living," a person might call in response to your voice mail, but you never left one. This message, in your voice, conveys the plans you were only considering. You contemplated calling, but never got around to it. These confused witnesses insist with confidence that the phantom call was never placed that day.

Other variations of chilling communications incorporate a "dead" person answering a call or picking up a phone when no one is at the house. This is oftentimes accompanied by devices that come to life while disconnected. Routine calls continue to occur, sometimes for years. For example, there was a case that involved a daily family call at 4 p.m., which continued undeterred by the death of the caller! Life's daily routine carried on as if the dead person remained unaware of their own passing. The two family members would talk for twenty minutes at a time. This lengthy phantom tradition lasted from 1959 to 1961. Perhaps they are not dead, if the multiverse is at work.

Other loved ones reach out on anniversaries or to warn of an impending family emergency, only to never connect again. Communication devices play a pivotal role in many hauntings, as phones and other electronics are key targets for paranormal manipulation.

Stories of successful connections motivated people to bury loved ones with their cherished cell phones in the hopes of one last call or text from beyond the grave. In a few rare occurrences, family wishes came true. Occasionally, "they" appear to require permission to make contact. Phantom callers explain that's the law, although no regard for breaking that law is expressed. No fear of punishment is expressed either.

UFO experiencers say the caller "mimics" a person. The message might include a warning not to share their encounters or an unnerving personal survey. The ghastly messages can contain strange beeping sounds and insect-like chattering voices.

What are the origins of these creepy messages? In many instances, it's the result of misinterpretation or lack of knowledge of the technology being used. In rare cases, it's coincidence disguised as meaningful signals within the noise that are too tempting to completely discount. And then there are the messages with witnesses and other contributory evidence that defy the usual explanations. The encounters featured in this book are hand-picked oddities that are provocative, bewildering, mysterious, and entertaining.

Omitted here are the multitude of cases that rely solely on an intermediary party, such as mediums, telepathic voices, visions, or EVP recordings. Instead, our journey focuses on *unexpected* messages received via *direct contact*.

2

UNKNOWN ENTITIES

The universe is under no obligation to make sense to you.
—Neil deGrasse Tyson

It's anybody's guess exactly who or what is behind these shocking communications, especially when it's tough to speculate the potential source at all. First-time messengers, known names, and unidentifiable voices keep us guessing. Positive and negative messages will spur theories to try to make sense of the unknown. These are categorized as the "unknown entities."

Entity Screams through the Radio
Sherryl Prelesnik
Grand Haven, Michigan, 1987

When Sherryl was sixteen years old, she left her grandmother's house in a 1975 Buick Electra Limited. She was driving fast with the radio blasting heavy metal. At the end of their dirt road was a set of train tracks for freight and commercial trains.

Sherryl explains,

As I got closer to the tracks, I heard a man's voice screaming on the radio over the song that was playing! He was yelling "Stop!" and it was coming right from the radio. The voice was so loud, it

The dirt road where the radio warning saved Sherryl's life.
Photo courtesy of Sherryl Prelesnik.

startled me. I realized I was too close to the train tracks. The yell was in time for me to realize the impending crash, so I slammed on my brakes and the car skidded to a halt—just as a train crossed my path. I sat there in the car for a while to compose myself and stop shaking. It was not in my mind. An actual voice from the radio was heard.

CHARACTERISTICS

MESSAGE TYPE: CAR RADIO (VOICE YELLED OVER A SONG)

FREQUENCY: ONCE

OTHER PHENOMENA: NO

FROM: UNKNOWN ENTITY

WITNESSES: NO

ELEMENTS: A WARNING THAT POTENTIALLY SAVED HER LIFE!

Ghost Computer Comes to Life
Sonny Taylor
Woodland Hills, California, 2015

My dad's side of the family was mostly unknown to me. I was a kid growing up without a dad in the Philippines. We only had contact with my aunt Mary and my half-brother Bruce during those times.

I didn't bother to check on Dad's family until I was in my thirties. My sister did most of the ancestry work, but abandoned it when she got too busy with her business.

One late night in early October of 2015, I felt a male presence, mostly out of the corner of my eye. This feeling repeated a few times until later that same month, when I had a sudden urge to find more about Dad's roots.

While searching online, I could still feel a presence right behind me. I came across a few names, but no further leads. Then, the page I was on froze. I hit the back button. Instead of going back, the page went forward. I was stunned at what I saw loaded on the screen: names of relatives and ancestral information that went on for quite a few pages.

The last page was about this pioneer in Coles County that came from Tennessee, the patriarch of the Taylor clan who served during the Battle of New Orleans.

I have since visited his grave and the battlefield he fought on. I have the feeling that the presence I felt two years ago was my great 4× grandpa, Michael Taylor. His youngest daughter was married to Abraham Lincoln's close cousin.

CHARACTERISTICS

MESSAGE TYPE: COMPUTER

FREQUENCY: ONCE

OTHER PHENOMENA: YES (FEELING A PRESENCE)

FROM: UNKNOWN ENTITY

WITNESSES: NO

ELEMENTS: PROVIDING HELP IN RESEARCH.

Mary, Mary: From Grave Photo to Car Radio
Bill Hall
Southington, Connecticut, 1984

In my college days, my magician friend Phil and I used to hang out in graveyards. We discussed and practiced magic and worked on great achievements, such as a way to vanish the moon. We also talked about the unknown since we were wonder-stricken by all of that—the debunking of fake practitioners like Uri Geller, along with mind-boggling urban legends and experiences that were interesting, yet often unverifiable.

One summer night in one favorite graveyard spot, we decided to try to contact the dead. Why not? We searched to find a perfect older grave for our experiment. We found the area that had photos of the departed on each gravestone. We found one. A younger woman. Her name was Mary, and she had long black hair and wore glasses.

Phil and I discussed exactly how we should go about this. It's an important discussion since we wanted the experiment to have the best chance of success. We decided to see if Mary could contact us through the car radio. We turned on the radio and turned the dial until we had thick static with no other stations bleeding through. In order to render our makeshift experiment viable, we decided to talk while the radio continued to play thick static. We wanted to make sure only static was playing for about twenty minutes before we proceeded.

After about a half hour, we started taking turns asking if Mary would show us she was there. Nothing happened. We continued talking about magic and let the radio continue to pump out thick white noise. As a last-ditch effort, we decided to shout out to Mary at the same time. By this time, the static had played for about an hour. Phil held up his hand and put a finger out and then another as we counted out to three, so our plea would be synchronized. On three, we shouted, "If you're there, Mary, tell us!" After the synchronized shout of "us" came out of our mouths, the static was completely gone, and we heard a lady's voice speak rapid, unintelligible words for about ten seconds and then it went right back to the static.

Despite being debunkers of countless phenomena, we stood dumbfounded. It really startled us. We ran to the car and shut the radio off and then we discussed it for some time after that. Our logical minds told us it was simply coincidence—and perhaps that's all it was. Certainly, statistically, that would appear to be the best explanation as opposed to something beyond the natural understanding of the world. Regardless, it is a night we'll never forget, leaving an impression that made me continue to seek out the paranormal.

Mary's graveyard home. *Photo by Bill Hall.*

CHARACTERISTICS

MESSAGE TYPE: CAR RADIO

FREQUENCY: ONCE

OTHER PHENOMENA: NO

FROM: STRANGER (MARY), CORRELATION WITHOUT CAUSATION?

WITNESSES: YES (FRIEND)

ELEMENTS: ELECTRONIC DISTURBANCE WITH SEEMINGLY SIGNIFICANT TIMING.

Talking through the Clock Radio
Jimmy Petonito
East Haven, Connecticut, 1989

This incident happened right around midnight after Diane's boyfriend left at about 11:45 p.m. She was twenty-five years old at the time and all alone in the house reading. Her parents were on vacation in Atlantic City, New Jersey.

Without warning, the AM/FM clock radio on the night table beside the bed came alive on its own, turned on, and a male voice—not a happy-sounding voice—yelled "Don't move!"

She looked at the radio startled and said, "What?!"

It yelled out again, "Don't move!"

She didn't know how to interpret it, but Diane took comfort in knowing that she would be moving out of the house within a week or two. Shaken, she immediately left the room and called her mom in Atlantic City, telling her what just transpired. Diane explained she was completely awake, so this was not an imagined incident.

Several times, the radio turned on by itself and through the static, a voice seemed to be trying to break through. Diane couldn't quite make out what was being said. It didn't sound like a radio station trying to come through either.

When Diane moved out, she left the AM/FM clock radio with her parents. A few years after Diane's mother passed away, she had another experience. She would periodically visit her dad and straighten up the house for him. She opened all the curtains and blinds in his bedroom to let the sun in and started to make his bed. Suddenly, the radio sprang to life again.

A woman's voice that sounded very pleasant came through the static and she understood it to say "It's okay, it's okay."

She was not scared this time. In fact, it made her feel quite comfortable. Diane said, "I hear you and I'm not afraid."

This is the AM/FM clock radio from which Diane heard voices.
Photo by Jimmy Petonito.

CHARACTERISTICS

MESSAGE TYPE: CLOCK RADIO

FREQUENCY: MULTIPLE

OTHER PHENOMENA: NO

FROM: UNKNOWN ENTITY, MOM

WITNESSES: NO

ELEMENTS: TWO DIFFERENT MESSENGERS VIA THE SAME CLOCK RADIO.

Gettysburg Ghosts Call to Play
Carla Pickett Hehir
Gettysburg, Pennsylvania, 2010

In 2010, my husband Daniel and I were staying at Round Top Campground in Gettysburg. We waited until later in the evening when it wasn't busy to go take showers at the bathhouse. The women's bathroom showers have a door on the left that you enter through, and the men's room has their shower doors on the right. The laundry room is in between.

Daniel and I agreed to meet in the laundry room when we were finished. As I showered, I felt as if I was being watched, but I was the only one there. When finished, I dressed and started brushing my hair at the mirror. I heard children laughing and running about in the laundry room.

Being overtired, I hesitated to go into the laundry room, because I just wanted quiet time. I decided to enter anyway and found the room empty. I told Daniel what I heard and felt and that, when he was finished with his shower, I wanted to return with my camera.

We went back to the RV, got the camera, and returned to the laundry room. The photos looked normal, but I kept feeling the presence of a young girl. I informed her that I was not going to hurt her and asked if she wanted to play. After a few minutes of nothing happening, we returned to the RV and went to sleep.

The next afternoon, I was with Daniel and speaking on the phone with my sister. Suddenly, in the middle of my sister's sentence, the line went silent. My sister's voice was replaced by the sound of a little girl merrily laughing and giggling. I immediately knew it was an identical match of the voice I heard in the bathroom the night before.

I asked, "Who is this?" trying to get her name.

She giggled and laughed again and then said, "Wanna play?"

Daniel was sitting so close that he also clearly heard the little girl. I was perplexed. I did realize what was happening at the moment, but it took me a few minutes for it to register and for my mind to grasp that this was really taking place.

The little girl's voice said, "I invited you."

Her words came slow and dragged out. It was a very eerie sound.

She continued, "I'm going home." This was followed by laughing and giggling again.

At once, I called my sister back. She didn't hear the little girl on the line. She only heard my voice the entire time. From my end, however, I couldn't hear my sister at all, just the little girl's voice.

CHARACTERISTICS

MESSAGE TYPE: LANDLINE PHONE

FREQUENCY: TWICE (ONCE BY PHONE, ONCE JUST VOICE)

OTHER PHENOMENA: YES (GETTYSBURG AREA)

FROM: STRANGER (LITTLE GIRL), UNKNOWN ENTITY

WITNESSES: YES (HUSBAND)

ELEMENTS: MET AT ONE LOCATION AND LATER INTERRUPTS THE PHONE LINE.

The South Shields Poltergeist
Marc and Marianne
South Shields, England, 2005

In 2005, strange things began happening to Marc and Marianne (pseudonyms) at their home in South Shields, England. In this case of poltergeist manifestation, the couple and their son were plagued by a variety of poltergeist activity including stacked chairs, doors closing, banging within the walls, and furniture moving of its own accord across the floor. It escalated by animating their three-year-old's toys to ghastly dance around the room, while other toys turned themselves on. An unseen force even threw toys at the terrified couple. One after another, toys were hurled at them while they remained in bed. They pulled the sheets over themselves to create a shield from the "living," flying objects. An invisible force retaliated by pulling the sheets off of them with a forceful yank. Marc ended up screaming and the activity stopped. His screams were not related to the toys, however; his back was in pain. They discovered he was left with thirteen scratch marks on his back from an unknown creature.

Mike Hollowell and Darren Ritson investigated this case and they came face to face with a peculiar entity and saw the poltergeist activity firsthand. It was a large, cold, negative, black, three-dimensional, blood-curdling silhouette. And then there were the bizarre text messages. They both expressed confidence that this was a genuine poltergeist case devoid of fraud.

Phantom messages were received as part of the overall phenomena. First, threatening messages were left on the son's magnetic doodle board. They were nasty, vulgar, and designed to intimidate and frighten:

"Die bitch!"

"You're dead."

"RIP."

Email and text messages followed with more vulgar taunting. The eerie email sender was untraceable. Marianne received death threats by text message on her cell phone too, such as "Going to die today."

There was no number displayed where the sender's phone number would customarily show. Marianne's home phone would also repeatedly call her cell phone at times when she knew no one was in the house to make the call. The poltergeist activity stopped on its own and there was no more activity ever since.

CHARACTERISTICS

MESSAGE TYPE: EMAIL, TEXT, MAGNETIC DOODLE BOARD

FREQUENCY: MULTIPLE

OTHER PHENOMENA: YES (POLTERGEIST INFESTATION)

FROM: UNKNOWN ENTITY (POLTERGEIST)

WITNESSES: YES (INVESTIGATORS)

ELEMENTS: NO "FROM" PHONE NUMBER WAS DISPLAYED, WHICH IS SOMETIMES AN ELEMENT OF PHANTOM CALLS.

From Graveyard to Facebook
Sean Austin
White Plains, New York, 2010

After investigating a house in which the stepfather allegedly killed his wife and stepdaughter—then himself—Sean started to feel he was being followed. He didn't know if it was negative or not. He started recording on a few different ghost box recorders to see if an EVP could provide a clue.

Sean asked, "Is someone following me?"

He played the recording back.

A female voice, claiming to be the murdered stepdaughter answered, "You freed me from my stepfather's hell. Thank you."

Sean was aware this might not be the stepdaughter at all, knowing that these parasites can simply lie.

One day, when Sean was working at his job at a wine store, a mother and her eight-year-old boy entered.

The little boy said to his mother, "There is a ghost there!"

The mother admitted that her son sometimes says things like that.

During the next few weeks, Sean and his friend Gregory explored cemeteries, looking for answers by asking more insightful questions. It seemed like the spirit of the stepdaughter was responding to Sean's questions. The female voice captured on audio was recognizable, sounding exactly like she did in prior communications. She answered questions wherever he went. Even in his apartment, he did EVPs.

She explained, "My stepfather is very angry with me for what I had done."

As Sean continued to gather a mounting number of recorded messages, he discovered the stepdaughter answered his questions before he verbally asked them out loud.

In addition to Sean obtaining conversations with her via EVPs, something much more surreal happened. The murdered stepdaughter sent him a friend request on Facebook. It was dated two months before she died.

Her random Facebook message simply said, "Nice eyes."

He found himself actively communicating with her via daily EVP recordings. She gave advice and held normal conversations. She even told Sean where his wallet was when he lost it.

Is this a strange case of contacting someone on Facebook "randomly" two months before being murdered and then connecting again from the graveyard? Did she know something about the future that we do not? Or did she know about the past and messaged Sean in retrospect from the future?

CHARACTERISTICS

MESSAGE TYPE: FACEBOOK (TWO MONTHS BEFORE BEING KILLED), EVP, TELEPATHICALLY

FREQUENCY: ONCE (ON FACEBOOK BEFORE DEATH), MULTIPLE OCCURRENCES VIA EVP/TELEPATHICALLY AFTERWARD

OTHER PHENOMENA: YES

FROM: UNKNOWN ENTITY, STEPDAUGHTER

WITNESSES: YES (INVESTIGATORS WORKING WITH SEAN)

ELEMENTS: GRAVEYARD SPIRIT SEEKING PEACE. POSSIBLE TIME SLIP PHENOMENON? FACEBOOK CONTACT FROM THE FUTURE TO THE PAST?

It Came through the Speakers
Linda Crouch
Hamden, Connecticut, 1985

Linda didn't live in a house that had any apparent paranormal activity, until the following occurrence happened at the age of fifteen.

Linda and her friend Jennifer got together at Linda's house to hang out after school. They started tossing out ideas of what they could do together. After different suggestions, they decided on making their own radio show. The two pretend stars decided to sing parody songs and be DJs. The process was to play albums later and then record it all back on a cassette tape recorder as one cohesive show.

The cassette tape recorder used was the small desktop style. Linda unwrapped and inserted a new cassette tape so their project could sound its best.

The disturbing phantom message came at around 3 p.m.

The two friends sat on the floor by the foot of Linda's bed, only a few feet from the record player. It was a simple one without a radio built in, but it did have two large speakers. The record player remained unplugged since they were going to record the music later for the show. Linda told us:

We were doing a little introduction to our pretend radio show when our attention was interrupted by an unusual sound. Through the unplugged record player speakers came a muffled song, almost like the sound a baby's mobile would make. It was "Home on the Range." I also would describe the sound like it was one of those windup music boxes playing it, which made it even creepier.

There were no lyrics. It was just an instrumental. The music played for only ten to fifteen seconds. The two startled teens looked at each other.

Jennifer said, "Lin? Lin?"

The two immediately ran down the stairs to her father, who was the only person home at the time. Since they were recording the show, they had it recorded on cassette tape.

They regained their composure and decided to brave a trip back upstairs to the bedroom. The tape was played back to see if the song was recorded. It was there, and they were excited. Then the recording turned stranger. A few seconds after you hear feet running down the stairs, a voice followed the eerie music.

Linda explains, "It sounded like a tortured voice saying. "Let meeeee ouuuuuuuuutt!" Just those three words but very stretched out. It was either a woman's voice or a child's voice and it sounded very far away. Still, the voice was clear enough for the words to be obvious."

Trying to be little detectives, they checked the plug to the record player and speakers just to make sure that they were unplugged. They were. The two looked at each other in disbelief.

Years later, Linda had another unusual experience. After Linda was married, the couple moved to the second floor of a three-family house that belonged in the family. Her grandmother lived on the first floor, and her aunt Clara lived on the third floor.

Periodically, the couple would argue, and Aunt Clara was always disturbed when they did. They could hear her yelling at them from upstairs. For a wedding present, Aunt Clara bought the couple a music box with two swans on top. She presented it by telling Linda that swans mate for life; they only have one partner. If their partner dies, they have been known to die from a broken heart.

Aunt Clara passed away in July of 1999. About a month later, the couple was arguing over something trivial. During the heat of their exchange, items began falling off the shelves. These items were nowhere near the edge and it seemed unlikely for them to just fall over. The two looked at each other in wonder. They immediately thought that Aunt Clara was not happy. On second thought, it also could just be their imaginations.

The next time they had an argument, items fell off the shelves again. Now they knew: It had to be Aunt Clara telling them to quit it. The final convincer was after all the items fell, music was heard. The swan music box with the doves started playing.

CHARACTERISTICS

MESSAGE TYPE: SPEAKERS (MUSIC FROM UNPLUGGED SPEAKERS), VOICE RECORDED, MUSIC BOX ACTIVATED

FREQUENCY: ONCE

OTHER PHENOMENA: NO (YEARS LATER, MAY OR MAY NOT BE RELATED)

FROM: UNKNOWN ENTITY, AUNT

WITNESSES: YES (FRIEND AND HUSBAND)

ELEMENTS: UNPLUGGED RECORD PLAYER, VOICE NOT HEARD REAL TIME BUT CAPTURED ON THE RECORDING

ELECTRONICS NOTE: ALTHOUGH IN THE OLDER ANALOG DAYS SPEAKER WIRES COULD ACT AS AN ANTENNA AND PICK UP TRANSMISSIONS, TODAY MANY TRANSMISSIONS ARE DIGITALLY ENCODED. SOME REMAIN ANALOG. THE UNUSUAL CAPTURE OF THE VOICE ADDS TO THE INTRIGUE OF THIS EXPERIENCE.

Wicked Whispers
Ed Dobalino
Newburgh, New York, 2012

Ed sat on his living room couch one day and heard whispering. He explained, "I couldn't place where it was coming from. I searched around to pinpoint its origin, but couldn't find the source."

A day or two later, he heard the strange voice again: "This time I was able to discover that it was coming from my living room TV. It was hard to tell if it was coming from the TV set or the cable box underneath it, because it seemed to be louder near the cable box."

As Ed leaned close to listen in to the voice, he was confident it was a male voice. "He" seemed to be repeating a phone number. Ed assumed it was a phone number due to the cadence of the message. The same numbers were repeated in a pattern. After the voice repeated the number several times, the unfriendly voice laughed.

Ed described the voice: "It was not a pleasant laugh. I considered it an evil laugh. That's how it felt."

He tried to record the voice, but the whispers were too soft to come through clearly. Ed listened intently, but still could not understand the negative voice or number, followed by the mocking laughter.

Ed confided, "I really didn't know what to do, and I couldn't understand what was going on. I unplugged both the cable box and the TV set. That didn't work. The voice still teased me by repeating the number sequence and then laughing."

This time, the voice was joined by a female voice. The two repeated the number sequence in unison. Then they both laughed together. This time the intent seemed even more clear.

"They both laughed in a sinister, shrieking manner that made me shake in terror," Ed shared.

He lived alone at the time, so Ed invited a neighbor to come over to hear the frightening laughing sounds. The neighbor was able to hear them, but also couldn't make out the numbers being chanted repeatedly, like out of a horror movie cult ritual.

Day or night, it didn't matter. At entirely random times, the whispering voices would suddenly shake him from his routine, and he would be forced to try again to investigate the source.

The relentless voices continued for about a week. It was eating away at Ed's sanity and he didn't feel comfortable in his own house. Out of ideas of what to do, he called the cable company to swap out the cable box hoping that would help. It did. Once the box was switched out, the whispering voices never disturbed Ed again—at least from the TV or cable box!

To this day, there are times that Ed is about to rest his head on the pillow when he hears the two tormenting voices whispering again to him. Are they now coming from the pillow? Or underneath? Ed doesn't know, but he has learned to adjust to knowing that the voices can be heard when they want to communicate. Perhaps one day they will clearly say what they need to say and leave him alone.

CHARACTERISTICS

MESSAGE TYPE: CABLE BOX

FREQUENCY: MULTIPLE

OTHER PHENOMENA: YES (THE VOICES CONTINUED AT A LATER DATE)

FROM: UNKNOWN ENTITY

WITNESSES: YES (NEIGHBOR)

ELEMENTS: ANOTHER CABLE BOX COMMUNICATION THAT LATER TAKES THE FORM OF COMMUNICATING WITHOUT IT.

On the Way to the Sanatorium
Cheryl Lynn Carter
Madison Heights, Michigan, 2017

At approximately 6 p.m on Thursday, November 16, 2017, I was driving alone on a desolate country road on my way to Hillsboro, Ohio, on business. John Cougar Mellencamp kept me company on the radio. The song "Jack and Diane" was playing.

When John sang, "Life goes on," I heard a man's voice come through the radio.

The voice asked, "Are you coming?"

Naturally, I thought there must be another radio station cutting in to the station I am listening to, so I didn't think anything unusual of it.

The song continued, and then the same man's voice came through the radio again. This time I heard the man say, "Cheryl, we are waiting for you!"

This was all on a Thursday. I had a paranormal investigation planned at St. Albans Sanatorium in Radford, Virginia, that coming Saturday evening. Built in 1892, it later became a sanitorium in the 1900s for the mentally ill.

Patients back then were subject to many questionable experimental procedures. Many of them died or committed suicide. They suffered insulin-induced comas, lobotomies, and a variety of other atrocities that left many of them far more damaged mentally. Some were even left for dead. The tragedies that occurred at this hospital created the perfect storm for a haunting. According to many, St. Albans is one of the most active haunted locations on the East Coast.

As soon as I heard the voices again, I instantly attributed it to St. Albans. It was a friendly, welcoming, middle-aged man's voice.

CHARACTERISTICS

MESSAGE TYPE: RADIO

FREQUENCY: TWICE

OTHER PHENOMENA: YES (IF YOU CONSIDER THE SANATORIUM)

FROM: UNKNOWN ENTITIES

WITNESSES: No

ELEMENTS: UNEXPECTED RADIO COMMUNICATION LATER LINKED TO A HAUNTED LOCATION.

The Rosenheim Poltergeist
Sigmund Adam
Rosenheim, Bavaria, 1967

Sigmund Adam's Rosenheim law office started experiencing weird phone line malfunctions. The calls started suddenly, for no visible reason. Employees would pick up, but no one was on the line. It was most unusual because all four of the office phones would ring simultaneously. Routine office calls would get cut off in the middle of conversations.

Adams concluded that the equipment was faulty, so he replaced the phones to fix the problem. But the determined other-realm pranksters continued to ring all the phones at once persistently. He called the phone company for help, and they sent a repair team out to look into the problem. The phone company thought the problem might be on the lines coming into the office since Adams already ruled out the phones themselves.

After examination of all the phone lines, no problem could be found.

New problems plagued office management. Adams began receiving charges for calls made to the speaking clock (in Germany, you can call for a recording of the current time). He was charged with placing six phone calls per minute to the speaking clock's number! He argued that it was physically impossible for him to dial that fast and have a call connected to register the charge.

Then the haunted office had other issues. The lights were acting as if they were alive. They would swing left and right by themselves and turn themselves on and off. This time, the power company was called and came out to check out the electrical circuits. Power surges were the assumed cause, so voltage meters were installed. Powerful surges were recorded, but no fuse was ever blown. Even the photocopier started to leak for some unknown reason.

Two physicists got word of the problems at the office and decided to try to help. However, after several visits to the office, they could not explain it either. Next, Hans Bender of Freiburg's Institute of Paranormal Research went to investigate. Hans noticed the timing of the phenomena matched when a young employee named Anne-Marie Scaberl was at the office. Activity often began soon after she arrived for the work day. When she left for the day, the place was absent of mayhem.

After talking to Anne-Marie, Bender concluded she was "a highly strung teenager with a lot of emotional turmoil. She held in a lot of anger; she hated her specific job, as well as the law office."

Poltergeist pandemonium heightened, as new disturbances of classic poltergeist antics were introduced: calendar pages ripped themselves off, paintings flew off office desks, and the employees thought the most shocking display was when a heavy oak cabinet (around 400 pounds) slid a few feet without damaging the linoleum.

Then Anne-Marie quit her job. The poltergeist activity quit too. The word on the street was the powerful poltergeist got a new job with her—the activity followed Anne-Marie. She later broke up with her fiancé, and more phenomena resulted. Finally, in 1969, she married and the poltergeist infestations ended.

It is important to remember that the majority of poltergeist activities usually center around children or teenagers (especially girls) or the phenomenon focuses on such environments where negativity thrives, such as abusive environments.

What happened in the city of Rosenheim was heavily documented.

CHARACTERISTICS

MESSAGE TYPE: LANDLINE PHONES

FREQUENCY: MULTIPLE

OTHER PHENOMENA: YES (POLTERGEIST)

FROM: UNKNOWN ENTITIES

WITNESSES: YES (EMPLOYEES, REPAIR TECHNICIANS, INVESTIGATORS)

ELEMENTS: RAPID DIALING AND PHONE MALFUNCTIONS TIED TO ANNE-MARIE'S OFFICE PRESENCE.

Elementary School Entities
Brenda Ozog
Westland, Michigan, 2013

Brenda works as a social worker at a local preschool that also provides special education. In the past, the building was used as an elementary school. In the 1960s, there was a brutal murder of two students. The janitorial staff told her stories about abnormal events happening late at night when they cleaned. Toys were found misplaced, as if abandoned after play by some interdimensional ghost children. Books flew all over the place of their own accord, and chairs screeched as they burst to life and moved weirdly across the floor. Others also experienced activity. One staff member told Brenda about an experience she had while walking through the school gym. The doors shook behind her. No one was there. Another staff member was held prisoner by an invisible force! She was found distraught in a locked closet and had to be let out. When asked how she got locked in, she simply thought someone locked her in. There was no other viable explanation, but no one was there to do the deed. Brenda is also a paranormal investigator. Through some recording sessions, she appeared to get confirmation of a spirit in the building. She was told it was a little boy.

By now, the office had acclimated to the paranormal mischief. Employees even named the ghost George, although no name was given during the sessions. Brenda also thinks there is an adult entity there too, but it's not active like George. Another antic joined the haunting: The water faucets turn on full blast at odd times when no one is there. The plumbers can't find any problem. An almost daily disturbance is a computer screen melting distortions as if the technology is being electrically attacked. The office clock often looks like the beginning to *The Twilight Zone*. The hands spin very fast until they spin out of control.

And then there are the office phones. They receive and make phantom calls! Brenda receives messages when she comes back from a break. One voice mail said, "Hello. . .hello. . .hello. . ." in a mesmerized odd monotone voice. Another example is a message that simply said, "Awww."

These are not calls cut short. There are no signs of interruption or static during the messages either. One call was from a creepy-sounding male

Brenda playing a phantom message for us that says "Brenda" in an unnatural robotic voice. *Video image by Bill Hall.*

voice that left a message that just said, "Brenda." The calls often display all zeros as the origination number.

The phantom also makes outgoing calls from other office phones. Doctor's offices and other various places receive calls from the other office phones that none of the employees made. The phone company is as confused as the plumbers.

Brenda noticed the difference with human energy being there. "George seems to get very active when we leave for holiday breaks. Upon returning, I find unusual messages on my phone. The return numbers, when not all zeros, don't work when I try to call back. To my knowledge, he has not tried to follow anyone home."

CHARACTERISTICS

MESSAGE TYPE: LANDLINE PHONES, COMPUTER (INTERFERENCE), VOICE MAILS

FREQUENCY: MULTIPLE

OTHER PHENOMENA: YES

FROM: UNKNOWN ENTITIES

WITNESSES: YES (SCHOOL STAFF)

ELEMENTS: INCOMING CALLS AND THE RARER OUTGOING PHANTOM CALLS.

The Real Story of "The Apartment/It Came from the Basement" from *The Scariest Night of My Life*

Michele Wilkins Palmieri
Middletown, Connecticut, 2017
Investigated by Jimmy Petonito and Laurene M. Gomez, MA, LMFT

Michele had been in her apartment for about a year. Her younger son was preparing to move in with his girlfriend, so she started to consider a smaller place. That's how this all began . . .

Michele explains, "I went to see an apartment, and when I arrived, a guy was packing up his stuff. I asked to take a quick look inside. He had a weird vibe about him. Something was *off*."

Upon eventually moving into that same apartment, Michele noticed there were red marks on the doorways and the apartment in front of hers had large bags of rice outside. She wondered why.

She described the apartment as beautiful and sunny, equipped with a quaint fireplace. Michele loved it. In April, on her son's birthday, the first evidence that something was very wrong surfaced. The family came over to take pictures, and they all gathered in various traditional family get-together poses.

"Then we looked at them all," Michele explained. Her mouth dropped. The faces of the family members were swirled and distorted in most of the photos.

In a few cases, there was an overpowering brightness, even though there was no obvious source of light and no flash setting used when taking the photos.

One day, Michele came home and her new water heater had busted. There was water everywhere; even her dog Milo was practically floating in his dog bed. Next, random black marks started to mysteriously appear all over the top and front of the washer and dryer. She tried to wash them off, but whatever the unknown substance was, it could not be removed.

In May, Milo began acting unusual. He didn't want to stay in the laundry room, even though that was his area when not with Michele in her bed (even there, Milo had to remain on guard duty).

Michele explains, "Milo and I were in bed, and I could hear something walking across the room. It then bumped into the bed frame! I could see Milo watching it as it neared the bed."

Another time, Michele heard Milo's squeaky toy make noise, as if stepped on. When she arrived at the laundry room, she found the toy in

Depiction of the black-winged gargoyle.
Illustration by Mike Mendes.

the center of the room. It was put away with all his toys in his toy basket, and Milo had not been in there. Michele was feeling trepidation about staying in the apartment.

The activity finally progressed enough to cause Michele to become filled with constant fear. One day, she reached into her closet and something was there. She felt it. And she saw it. "It looked like a gargoyle. Its skin was many layered and rubbery. Then I saw its wings. It was overwhelming. The face was long and pointed, and the expression was one that caused terror. That's the best way I could describe it."

One night, she heard howling unlike anything she's every heard before. It came from the woods in the direction of the patio off the living room.

Michele thinks back to the experience: "It sounded like something in pain. I also heard galloping through the thick woods in the distance. It was no dog or horse, that I know. Besides, a horse can't gallop through that area; it's not clear enough for that."

There was more to deal with than the apartment or the woods. The apartment upstairs was beginning to become a new problem. The construction noise was unbearably loud, and Michele grew concerned about their disrespectful work schedule. Even during acceptable hours, the noise was deafening. Her complaints were responded to and the answer only made Michele angrier: No one was in that apartment and no construction or repairs were going on! That took time to sink in. No one up there? No construction? What was all that noise then? The same creature in that apartment? Michele couldn't believe that no one was up there, so maintenance had to provide proof. They brought her up to the apartment and unlocked the door. She stepped inside to get to the bottom of the mystery. It was empty, and it was clear that there was no work in progress of any kind in the entire apartment.

Back at Michele's place, the haunting continued. A malevolent force made the shower curtain come to life and wrap around her while showering. Later that night, the entity tried to touch her in bed. "It's like it was trying to see how far I would let it go," Michele said.

One night in October, the bed started shaking uncontrollably. Someone— or some thing—was shaking the bed! The time was 3 a.m. Milo was staring up in space at the invisible creature. Then the ominous presence triggered the outdoor motion light. After a few minutes, the ordeal was over. Michele got out of bed and called her sister, thinking it was a seizure. Her sister rushed right over. Since her sister couldn't calm her jitters, Michele was taken to the emergency room. This was serious. She was seeing the impossible before her eyes—strange things that no healthy person should be seeing. Despite her detailed account of her experiences, nothing wrong was found.

Back home, her flip phone had a new message on it. Upon playback, she heard her younger son's name (Caleb). Then, names of people closest to her were spoken. And then that unforgettable creature of terror appeared again. It was persistent. The hideous gargoyle creature lurked in the corner of the door, watching. Michele was fully awake; this was no sleep paralysis. Milo was responding as well during these sightings; he would crouch in fear during each loathsome visit.

Other paranormal indicators were ever present. Her son's room was freezing all the time, in an otherwise warm apartment.

December arrived, and it was time to decorate. The nativity set and candles were added to the mantel, but they didn't remain there for long. The items flew off and crashed to the floor. And the old flip phone was calling again. This time it was a message with the voice of a boy. Jimmy and Bill heard the recording of this message. It sounded like a xylophone (for the sake of trying to describe the sound).

It's a small child singing, "Don't worry about you baby . . ."

It was time to call someone for help. Michele called Laurene M. Gomez and asked her if she believed in ghosts. She answered yes.

Laurene arrived with Jimmy at the apartment, and they started to investigate.

Jimmy recalls a most interesting experience: "Michele's little flip phone was getting recordings in response to her questions. I had three different recorders and was getting nothing."

I asked out loud, "How come you won't give me an answer when I ask a question?"

On playback, a voice said, "You are a jerk."

That is the only response Jimmy was able to obtain. They advised Michele to do the asking. The important question to ask was: "What do you want from Michele?"

The response came with a name: Luther. Research revealed a farming family on the land before the apartments were built. Although Luther was

Jimmy Petonito and Bill Hall with Laurene M. Gomez, MA, LMTF, and Michele
Wilkins Palmieri (lower right). *Photo by Jimmy Petonito.*

a common name, one family story stood out: A man named Luther died,
and his wife remarried and had a baby named Luther.

The recordings continued. Jimmy played back a recording that said,
"She's dead." It was very clear. Jimmy didn't want to frighten Michele, so
he told her the voice said, "Cheese head."

Laurene and Jimmy decided to do a blessing. They both could feel that the
laundry room was an important area. Michele also had a new computer in there
that mysteriously burned out. The two assured Michele she would be alright.

Comforted by the visit and reassurance, Michele turned in and was
starting to settle in to bed. Her peace was disturbed by a painful burning
in her upper chest.

"I sat up and I saw lines forming while it was burning into me. I yelled
to my son to come look at them. There was a line of four scratch marks."

Sleep did not come easy or for long that night. Early the next morning,
Laurene received her delayed distress call. Michele was thinking about moving.

One night, while trying to drift off to sleep, she was rattled by the feeling of a presence above her. "It hovered over me. It was dark. Again, I felt like I was being tested as to how far I would let it go. The leathery creature brushed against my leg, and the foreign touch slid up my leg, touching me continuously until it reached my knee. Then it stopped."

There was an indentation on the bed. Michele knew she was not alone. Other times, the visitor was less grimacing. A man with long gray hair was seen visiting. Always wearing a black leather jacket with black pants, he didn't look at all from our world. As we often say in the paranormal to describe these instincts, something was "off" about him.

She was given rosary beads and kept them in hopes of protection. Responding to a noise in the bedroom, Michele ventured into the room to investigate. The rosary beads were missing. After searching around, the beads were discovered underneath the bed arranged in a perfect circle. And there was something else: The beads had changed color, becoming darker than before.

The unorthodox ways of the neighbors became clear. After additional research, the mystery of the red marks on the doorways was solved; certain religions do that in order to keep the spirits out. And large bags of rice also were a deterrent to the "creature." This cultural protection stopped the evil spirits from entering because they would have to stop to count the rice. They couldn't help themselves. Who knew they had OCD?

Obviously, it was time to move. After leaving the apartment and settling into a new place, Michele reported a few more run-ins with the black-winged shadow creature. It followed her for a while. On one occasion, when getting ready for work, she came face to face with the smirking gargoyle waiting outside the bedroom. The grotesque beast took flight. The wings expanded fully as it flew by. The entity's dark form blocked out the light as it flew overhead. After that, Michele admits she got busy with other things. It appeared the creature no longer warranted her attention. She didn't want to play anymore and deserved a fresh start.

"At times, it seems to draw me back to the apartment. It's hard to explain," Michele confessed. Jimmy, Laurene, and I understood. It's not uncommon for this type of encounter.

Michele was also finally able to learn her son's experience of those days too. Her son felt and heard many things that he wouldn't be able to discuss for years. They both could feel when things were "off." At a yard sale that extended into the house, they walked into a bedroom where items were on display.

The two locked eyes and her son said, "Do you want to get out of here?"

Michele asked if it was an estate sale and got the answer yes.

"There is an old lady with a bun in her hair and she is pissed," she announced. Then they made their exits.

(See Chapter 13 for a bonus case with a black-winged shadow creature.)

CHARACTERISTICS

MESSAGE TYPE: FLIP PHONE, VOICE MAILS

FREQUENCY: MULTIPLE

OTHER PHENOMENA: YES (HAUNTING, POSSIBLE FLAP AREA)

FROM: UNKNOWN ENTITIES (BLACK-WINGED SHADOW GARGOYLE CREATURE AND OTHERS)

WITNESSES: YES (INVESTIGATED BY JIMMY AND LAURENE M. GOMEZ)

ELEMENTS: BLACK-WINGED SHADOW CREATURE AND OTHER ACTIVITY. IT SOUNDS LIKE A POTENTIAL FLAP AREA WHERE THIS NEGATIVE PARASITE WAS ABLE TO FEED OFF MICHELE UNTIL SHE BROKE THE FREQUENCY CONNECTION.

3

People You Know: Warnings, Help, Hello

It's funny how most people love the dead.
Once you're dead, you're made for life.
—Jimi Hendrix

Sure, we would love to hear from them. Grandpa, Mom, Dad, children, friends—they all *appear* to visit. But is it really them? Are they alive in another universe or dimension? Are they dead? Or is something else altogether happening that we haven't dared imagine yet?

These phantom messages include warnings of things to come, reaching out to help others, and some just pop-in to say hello on an otherwise boring day. Certainly, some of these cases might be bereavement hallucinations, especially if experienced within a mourning period. There are obvious effective methods to explain them away. It's harder when there are witnesses. Although we often misinterpret what we experience, the phenomena in this category presents some compelling testimony. Therefore, they may forever remain unsolved.

The Deceased Borrows a Cell Phone
Bella Reynolds
Silsbee, Texas, 1984

My husband's grandfather passed away back in 1984. Grandpa Reynolds comes to visit, and every time he does, he calls my cell phone from my husband's cell phone. He hangs up and then he calls back. This is a repeated pattern. He calls as least once a month and calls from my husband's personal cell phone and also from his work cell phone. There have been a couple of voice mails, but I can't hear anything even with my earbuds in.

My bloody house is so active with family members. Since the hurricane, I've had even more visitors. It's always a circus here.

I also have a set of twins. They sit on my couch and argue about baseball. I have no idea who they are, but their names are Timmy and Tommy Thibodaux. They wear white shrimper's boots.

CHARACTERISTICS

MESSAGE TYPE: CELL PHONE

FREQUENCY: MULTIPLE

OTHER PHENOMENA: YES

FROM: GRANDPA

WITNESSES: YES (HUSBAND AND WIFE)

ELEMENTS: THIS PLACE POTENTIALLY COULD BE IN A FLAP AREA. GRANDPA WAS THE ONLY FAMILIAR "GHOST," AND THE REST WERE UNFAMILIAR IDENTITIES.

The Haunted Clock Radio
Jolie Cole
Snellville, Georgia, 1980s

At age thirteen, Jolie's grandmother was living with the family due to complications from diabetes. On the morning of her passing, it was business as usual for Jolie's school preparation. She ate breakfast and then went to hug her grandmother as she always did before leaving for school. Grandma was not feeling well but made a smile for her lovely granddaughter. But her usual well wishes for the day were different this time. Ominous perhaps.

She said, "I love you, don't ever forget that."

Her alarm clock was going off and she didn't want to go downstairs to turn it off, so she asked Jolie to do that for her. She did.

During the morning break at school, Jolie had a feeling that her grandmother had died. When she left school to catch the bus, her dad was waiting there. He said the words she feared most: "Grandma passed away." She was only fifty-two years old.

Jolie moved downstairs into her grandma's old room. She always had a feeling of comfort and safety in that room, especially when missing her grandmother. Jolie left Grandma's unplugged digital clock on a dresser in her room as a token of remembrance.

As the first Christmas without Grandma was approaching, Jolie was missing her and thought about her often. After coming home from seeing a movie with friends, she started on her homework and then went off to bed around 2 a.m. Suddenly, the silence of her room was broken by lively static from her grandmother's digital clock. It was glowing green like it did when turned on. Jolie looked over to the radio and it was indeed on! Her grandmother's voice filled the room from the radio. "I love you, don't forget."

"I turned the light on and went over to the radio and it turned off. I checked the plug and it was as I suspected: not plugged in," Jolie recalled.

On Christmas morning, she woke to find three presents under the tree from her grandmother. She had purchased them in September, and Jolie's mom found them in her cedar chest when she cleaned it out. Her grandmother was not done communicating.

I honestly believe, with both occurrences, that my grandmother was letting me know she is still around and checking on me. I always wished she would have been here to meet her great-grandchildren. To this day, I still receive signs that she is near—a faint smell of her White Shoulders perfume. Yes, I remember that she loves me.

CHARACTERISTICS

MESSAGE TYPE: CLOCK RADIO (UNPLUGGED)

FREQUENCY: MULTIPLE

OTHER PHENOMENA: No

FROM: GRANDMA

WITNESSES: No

ELEMENTS: MOVING TO GRANDMA'S OLD ROOM IS INTERESTING. ELECTRONICS WORKING WITHOUT BEING PLUGGED IN.

Calls from an Abandoned Office
Bob
Bridgeport, Connecticut, 2010

Bob is not involved with the paranormal. After his father died, he received a call from the General Electric service shop where his dad worked for thirty-five years. That sounds normal, but there is a twist; the shop closed soon after his father retired. The call originated from his father's old extension, 2618. The building was completely empty, and for security purposes, General Electric bolted all the exits shut and shut off the phone and electrical service. Bob told us, "I have no idea what happened. I am content thinking that Dad might just be saying hello to his boy."

CHARACTERISTICS

MESSAGE TYPE: LANDLINE PHONE

FREQUENCY: ONCE

OTHER PHENOMENA: No

FROM: DAD

WITNESSES: No

Vanishing Patient from Room 18
Jennifer Bergeson
Vernon, Connecticut, 2003

Jen didn't know her grandmother well. Being adopted, neither did her mother. Nevertheless, she always seemed to be watching over them.

In 2003, Jen's mother visited a psychic named Naomi. She didn't provide much information, other than a message that was "coming through" particularly strong.

Naomi saw a tall, dark-haired woman holding a baby. Jen's mother interpreted that to be her mother, and the baby her sister. While still a baby, her sister tragically drowned in the bathtub.

The psychic told her the lady was giving one message: "Life is not long, life is short."

The dark-haired woman pointed at her mom while delivering the message.

Fast forward to 2010. Jen is thirty-seven and working as a phlebotomist in a trauma center at St. Luke's Hospital in Cedar Rapids, Iowa.

"We often received alerts from the overhead speaker system for stroke and sepsis alerts. When you heard those messages, you immediately hurry to the room that generated the alert. Usually the room is full of medical personnel," Jen explained.

On Saturday morning, around 11 a.m., Jen received an alert for room 18. When she arrived at the room, something struck her as odd: There were only two nurses, not the usual assembly of emergency assistance. A nurse was in the process of pulling a white sheet up to the patient's chest. The other nurse was at the computer station.

Looking at the nurse by the bed, she asked, "Am I in the right room?" The nurse said, "Yes. You're right where you're supposed to be."

Just then, the nurse walked out of the room. Jen thought that was odd too. Coworkers and friends acted strange. It was almost as if they didn't know her.

Responding to the sepsis alert, Jen prepped to obtain blood cultures. As she went about her routine, she glanced over to the old man on the bed. He was extremely pale, in his seventies, and sported long white hair with a matching white beard. He was unresponsive. Jen could barely see his chest move beneath the sheet. She feared he was close to death.

She put the tourniquet tightly onto his arm. He didn't blink; he wasn't looking at all. As she readied the needle for his arm, he suddenly shot upright in the bed and looked into her eyes.

Jen put her left hand on his right shoulder and comforted him. "You're in the ER. I just need to do some blood work on you."

He reacted by lifting his left arm and pointing his long bony finger directly at her face and spoke, "You think life is long. It's not. Life is short!"

The strange patient encounter. *Illustration by Mike Mendes.*

Settling back down, she drew his blood. Jen explains,

This man came in as a John Doe, so I had to scan his wristband to keep all of his information in the main database. I scanned each test given, so we could later manually enter the results when that information is received back. I sent the blood to the lab through a system of tubes, like the ones the banks used. Still bothered by his cryptic words, I went over to the nurse's station for about ten minutes. The same nurse was there that was in the room earlier with me.

"Hey, Jen, how are you?" she asked.

The nurse acted completely different from when they were in the old man's room earlier. Across the hall from there, Jen could see clearly into room 18. There was an empty, freshly made bed. No patient was there.

Jen inquired, "Where is the man that was just in that room? What's going on with him?".

The nurse responded, "He's been gone for three or four hours."

That couldn't be. Jen was in that room with the man less than ten minutes ago!

Confused, Jen explained what happened next: "I ran down to the laboratory to check on the samples I sent down there. The cultures, tubes, records—we looked to find them but there was nothing to be found."

In 2011, Jen found herself back in Connecticut working at St. Francis Hospital in Hartford. She suffered a breakup and left her job and house behind. Those were hard times.

Jen told us, "I was texting my mom on break at one of the lowest points in my life. A picture of my grandmother was received during our texting conversation."

Jen replies, "Mom, that's a great picture of grandma! It's my favorite."

Mom texts back, "I didn't send that. I don't even have that picture on my computer or my cell phone!"

An instant mystery was before them. Jen knew *she* didn't sent the photo. Someone else did. Or no one did? It just showed up.

"We never could figure out how that picture appeared on our phones. Knowing what I was going through at the time, I understood this to mean it's my grandmother telling me I'm not alone and everything's going to be okay because she is here with me."

A picture of Jennifer's grandmother. *Photo courtesy of Jennifer Bergeson.*

CHARACTERISTICS

MESSAGE TYPE: TEXT (OF A PHOTO)

FREQUENCY: ONCE

OTHER PHENOMENA: YES (AT THE HOSPITAL)

FROM: GRANDMA

WITNESSES: YES (JEN AND HER MOM)

ELEMENTS: COMFORT WHEN NEEDED APPEARS TO BE THE GOAL OF SENDING THE PHOTO. THE HOSPITAL PHENOMENA ARE VERY INTERESTING AND COULD BE ATTRIBUTED TO A FEW THINGS. ONE FAVORITE POSSIBILITY IS A TIME SLIP.

Impossible Voice Mail and Texts
Andrea Mesich
Detroit, Michigan, 2005

After a long battle with cancer, Andrea's dad, John, passed away in 2005. Approximately one month after John's death, Andrea and her mom went out and bought a new digital answering machine. Prior to that, they always had an answering machine that used a cassette tape to record the incoming messages.

They came home the next day to find the new machine's message indicator light blinking. (This was the first message they received on this new answering machine.) The two went over and played the message. There was nothing but loud static for about two minutes. They looked at each other, wondering about the message, and then they heard a voice. It was Andrea's dad's voice . . . but how could that be?

Andrea, not believing what she just heard, looked at the number and it came up unknown. She then asked her brothers to come to the house and listen for themselves. John and Andy both came over at different times that day to listen to the message. Without being told who they thought it was, the message was played for them to hear. Both brothers instantly said the same thing: It was obviously their deceased father.

Through the static, their dad's voice broke through and said, "I love you." Then they heard another voice say, "That's the light, let's go."

Andrea relayed that there was other phenomena that started after her brother Andy went to Gettysburg and brought back some rocks as souvenirs. Ever since then, there's been paranormal activity in the house, such as sounds of boots walking or marching.

Andy got an instant message on AOL from the name "John Mesich." Andy assumed it was his brother John, because his father (also named John), was deceased.

The instant message said, "The lightning is beautiful here."

He was confused by this because he knows there were no storms around and didn't understand why his brother would have sent this.

Andy called his brother John and asked what he meant by the message. John didn't get back to him for a while since he is a police officer and was on a traffic stop at the time. When he did reply, he had no idea about any message—he hadn't sent one. Andy went back to the screen to take a picture of the instant message, but it was gone.

Andrea told us she believes that some attachment was brought home from Gettysburg, and perhaps her dad was helping them. After that call from "Dad," all paranormal activity stopped. She listened to the message often, but eventually it was lost either due to auto delete or something else related to the new digital technology.

Before this odd experience, Andrea was not interested in the paranormal. After experiencing her dad calling and leaving a message, she was motivated to find answers and became a paranormal investigator.

CHARACTERISTICS

MESSAGE TYPE: VOICE MAIL, TEXT

FREQUENCY: ONCE

OTHER PHENOMENA: YES (GETTYSBURG FLAP AREA)

FROM: DAD

WITNESSES: YES (ANDREA; HER MOTHER, CLAIRE; HER BROTHER, ANDY; AND HER BROTHER, JOHN)

ELEMENTS: THE MESSAGE ON THE SCREEN DISAPPEARS.

Train Crash Victim Calls Loved Ones Thirty-five Times
Charles Peck
San Fernando Valley, California, 2008

On September 12, 2008, at 4:22 p.m. in California's San Fernando Valley, a commuter train going eighty-three miles per hour collided with a freight train. There were 225 people aboard. It became known as the "Chatsworth crash." One hundred and thirty-five people were injured and twenty-five died. The engineer was busy texting and failed to yield to a red signal. The train ended up on the other track facing off to a Union Pacific freight train coming from the opposite direction.

Charles E. Peck, a forty-nine-year-old customer service agent for Delta Air Lines, went to Los Angeles for a job interview at Van Nuys Airport. His goal was to be close to his fiancée, Andrea Katz of Westlake Village. The couple was holding off on marriage until they were living in the same state.

Andrea, along with Peck's parents and siblings, heard news of the crash on the radio as she was driving to the train station to pick him up. Naturally, they were quite grief stricken by the news.

Metro Link crash. *Photo licensed under a Creative Commons Attribution-Share Alike 3.0 United States License.*

It took twelve hours to recover Charles's body from the wreckage. For the long hours prior, however, Peck's cell phone made call after call to his loved ones. It called his son, his brother, his stepmother, his sister, and Andrea. A friend who lived in the same complex as Charles also received a call. In total, thirty-five calls had been made throughout the course of the night!

Whenever they answered these unexplainable calls, they heard static. They tried calling back, but their calls went straight to his voice mail. They thought Charles was trapped and trying to use his cell phone to call for help. The slew of calls were relayed to authorities. The emergency crew attempted to find the phone through its signal. They checked the remains left behind in the first train where the calls were originating from. They found no phone anywhere despite thoroughly searching the train car and calling the phone's number. Rescue crews found Charles's body around midnight—an hour after the calls stopped. Based on his severe injuries, there was no question that he died on contact.

Skeptics would say that he must not have died on contact and made the calls before dropping the phone. But Charles was in the very first car. The doctor said he was killed instantly upon being jolted from the car at the time the two trains crashed. Not only was it impossible for him to stay alive for hours making phone calls, he would not have survived for even one whole minute after impact. With that theory disproven, all that was left were the strange repeated calls to different family members after he was already dead. The cell phone was never recovered, and no one is sure how the calls were made from a train car that was *not* occupied and had no living survivors near it. Everyone was questioned and no one made the calls. But someone—or something—did.

CHARACTERISTICS

MESSAGE TYPE: CELL PHONE

FREQUENCY: MULTIPLE (A TOTAL OF THIRTY-FIVE CALLS THROUGHOUT THE NIGHT)

OTHER PHENOMENA: NO

FROM: FAMILY MEMBER (CHARLES)

WITNESSES: YES (THE FAMILY MEMBERS WHO RECEIVED THE CALLS)

ELEMENTS: THE CELL PHONE WAS NEVER FOUND. THAT'S UNFORTUNATE BECAUSE IT MAY HAVE REVEALED MORE CLUES OR MORE QUESTIONS ABOUT HOW HIS PHONE MADE ALL THOSE CALLS TO LOVED ONES. IN OTHER WORDS, HIS MECHANIC, HAIR

STYLIST, DENTIST, OR DOCTORS MADE UP NONE OF THE OUTGOING DIALS THROUGHOUT THE NIGHT. IT WAS JUST HIS LOVED ONES, WHO WERE NOT LOCATED NEAR EACH OTHER ON HIS CONTACT LIST. ALTHOUGH THERE IS NO CONCRETE TIE TO THE PERSON (THEY DIDN'T TALK WHEN THE PARTY PICKED UP, FOR EXAMPLE), IT REMAINS AN IMPRESSIVE MYSTERY.

Dead Friend's Emails Predict the Future
Jack Froese
Dunmore, Pennsylvania, 2011
Courtesy of Historic Mysteries website

Jack died from a fatal heart arrhythmia. Naturally, his family and friends were devastated by his death since he was just thirty-two years old. After about five months, emails began to be received from Jack's old email account. Tim Hart, one of Jack's closest friends, received emails entitled, "I'm Watching." The body of the email reminisced discussions the two shared several months before Jack died. The email also contained this shocking revelation: "Did you hear me? I'm at your house. Clean your f***ing attic!!!!"

Tim was very concerned when he read the unexpected email. He was speechless and disturbed. "I turned ghost white when I read it. It was very quick and short but to a point that only Jack and I could relate on," Hart told the BBC, adding that shortly before Froese's death, he privately teased Hart about the attic's messy state. They were up there considering the potential for finishing it off when the dirty attic comment was made. Hart later sent a reply to the account, but has yet to get a response.

Tim didn't think anyone but the two of them would know about those private conversations that were shared in the puzzling emails. It was unthinkable that someone would use Jack's old email account.

Jack's cousin Jimmy McGraw also received an email from his old account. This time the message was more unsettling. After Jack died, Jimmy broke his ankle. The email read: "Hey Jim, how ya doing? I knew you were going to break your ankle. Tried to warn you. Gotta be careful. Tell Rock for me. Great song, huh? You're welcome. Couldn't get through to him. His [blanked out] didn't work."

Jimmy was convinced that his cousin was keeping an eye on him, but he had to admit that the chances it was really him were remote. What happened here? Who sent the emails? There were no signs of the account being hacked and no one knew his password to the account. One could argue it was one of those new services that will send timed emails on your behalf after your death. Jack died suddenly, however, so that is not likely. Even if he did, he would have needed someone to find out about the ankle injury and incorporate it into the email.

CHARACTERISTICS

MESSAGE TYPE: COMPUTER (EMAIL)

FREQUENCY: TWICE

OTHER PHENOMENA: NO

FROM: FRIEND (JACK)

WITNESSES: YES (TIM AND JIMMY AND SAVED EMAILS)

ELEMENTS: AN EMAIL WAS SENT TO TWO DIFFERENT LOVED ONES. INSIDE INFORMATION ABOUT THE INJURY WAS INCLUDED. A SUGGESTION OF KNOWING THE FUTURE IS INCORPORATED.

Buried with Her Cell Phone
Frank Jones
Lancashire, England, 2008
Courtesty of the *Blackpool Gazette*

A man from Lancashire whose house has a reputation for poltergeist activity claims he's being haunted by text messages from his dead wife, the *Blackpool Gazette* reported in a March 27, 2008 article entitled "Man Believes Dead Wife Is Contacting Him on Mobile."

Twelve years ago, fifty-nine-year-old Frank Jones had his home on Windsor Avenue, Thornton, exorcised after a malevolent spirit dubbed "The Thing" had already driven one terrified family from the house. Now it turned its attention on Frank and his wife and children.

In 1971, the previous residents (the Ross family) told the *Gazette* how The Thing had "pulled at their bed covers while they were asleep" and they "sensed a vile smell and felt something breathing in their ears."

Jones moved in twenty years ago, solidly skeptical about the legendary presence, but "soon changed my mind."

He recounted:

I just thought they were imagining it. But there was a lot of banging and an earthy smell in the house. Then one night, I was lying in bed and a mist came across the room. I wanted to shout out at it, but I couldn't get any words out. My face seemed to be paralyzed. It all got too much for me when that happened.

Jones's thirty-year-old daughter Maureen confirmed that "The Thing" turned on faucets and thoroughly ransacked the house.

In deep thought, she said:

You think people are exaggerating until you experience it. I was home alone one evening and suddenly heard these footsteps coming up the stairs. They went into my dad's bedroom and then I heard all of the cupboards banging open. It sounded like burglars.

An exorcist from Fleetwood Spiritualist Church attempted to cleanse the property of the spirit they thought was trapped between two worlds.

Peace then reigned at Windsor Avenue until five years ago, when Jones suffered a double tragedy: the death of his son Steven, thirty-two, from a brain tumor, and wife Sadie, sixty-nine, three months later from a heart attack.

Jones explained:

Just after Sadie died, I came home and I felt like I didn't want to go in the house. I got a missed call on my mobile, but it didn't ring. The call was from my own home number, but there was no one in the house. When I went inside, there was the smell of cigarettes (which Sadie used to smoke) and the smell of her perfume.

Jones says his family has since received strange SMS messages, which they believe to be from Sadie.

He concluded: "She always had a mobile with her. We buried her with her phone. There have been messages with words Sadie would say but there's never a number."

Characteristics

Message Type: Landline phone (calls from home when no one is there), text

Frequency: Multiple

Other Phenomena: Yes (haunting phenomena, smell of her cigarettes and perfume)

From: Wife (Sadie)

Witnesses: Yes (Jones family and Ross family)

Elements: She called from the house when no one was home. This was followed by multiple texts. She was buried with her phone. No phone number showed.

If Pictures Could Talk
JoAnn Jordan
Madison, Connecticut, 1990

About ten years ago on my birthday, I was feeling sad. I deeply missed my mom, who passed away in 1990. I miss her every birthday, holiday, or other treasured family occasion.

In the bathroom, there is a picture frame that has a feature where you can record audio and then press a button and hear the recorded message. This was a gift from my husband and children. I kept a photo of my three children in the frame, and when you press the button, it says, "Happy Mother's Day, Mommy! We love you."

The recorded message would not play unless you pressed the button on the frame. While scrubbing the bathroom floor, I heard audio come from the nearby picture frame's speaker that said, "Happy birthday." It was a woman's voice. I couldn't exactly identify the voice, but I'd like to think it was Mom since I was thinking of her and missing her. The picture frame never spoke again.

CHARACTERISTICS

MESSAGE TYPE: AUDIO PICTURE FRAME

FREQUENCY: ONCE

OTHER PHENOMENA: No

FROM: MOM

WITNESSES: No

ELEMENTS: THE FRAME ACTIVATES BY ITSELF AND HAS A NEW RECORDED MESSAGE.

Uncle's Answering Machine Message
Dawn A. Mitchell
Garden City Park, New York, 1995

In June of 1995, we were at a dinner celebration for my uncle Ivan, who had passed away a few months earlier at only fifty-eight years old. His wife, Delores (my aunt), and all of our children were together for the big dinner.

After eating, we returned to my house. Everyone who attended the dinner came back to my house, except a few of the children.

The answering machine was blinking with three brand new messages. The first two were just friends of mine. The third message gave us chills and left us speechless. It was my uncle Ivan's voice on the answering machine singing "Como Fue"—my aunt's favorite song.

CHARACTERISTICS

MESSAGE TYPE: ANSWERING MACHINE

FREQUENCY: ONCE

OTHER PHENOMENA: NO

FROM: UNCLE (IVAN)

WITNESSES: YES (THE PEOPLE AT THE FAMILY GATHERING)

ELEMENTS: ANNIVERSARY CALL. THEY WERE HOLDING A CELEBRATION FOR HIM.

Interaction over the Intercom
Sherryl Prelesnik
West Haven, Connecticut, 2001

On October 12, 2001, when at work in West Haven, Connecticut, I was putting together posters for an upcoming open house.

At around 2 p.m., a woman's voice made an announcement over the loud speaker: "Harriett Cooper, please call the operator. Harriett Cooper, please call the operator."

I smiled, lifted my head, and thought to myself, *That is Grandma's name.* It was strange because the announcement was abnormally loud. I thought perhaps the lady just turned up the volume all the way. I didn't think about the incident for the rest of the day. The next day, Saturday, at around noon, I received a call from my mother. She was clearly upset, and I could tell she had been crying. I asked her what was wrong.

Clearly shaken, she told me, "Your grandmother went into a coma yesterday. I'm sorry for waiting so long to tell you but I couldn't call yesterday."

At that moment, the announcement from the day before flooded my thoughts.

I asked Mom, "Do you know when she went into the coma? Do you know the time?"

My mom said, "That's a strange question. Why do you ask?"

I didn't answer. I couldn't help but repeat the question. She said "Well, it was around 2 p.m."

I sat there in shock, then told her what happened the day before. Without hesitating, I quickly said, "Well, I guess she called the operator."

In unison, we both laughed and cried. My grandmother passed away three days later, on October 16, 2001.

CHARACTERISTICS

MESSAGE TYPE: INTERCOM (ANNOUNCEMENT)

FREQUENCY: ONCE

OTHER PHENOMENA: NO

FROM: GRANDMA

WITNESSES: NO

ELEMENTS: A WARNING? THE TIME OF THE COMA COINCIDED WITH THE PHANTOM MESSAGE PHENOMENA.

Dad Kept His Promise
Michele Wilkins Palmieri
Middletown, Connecticut, 2017

On February 1, 2017, Michele's dad Silas passed away at eighty-one years old. For decades, he worked at an aircraft parts manufacturing plant where he was exposed to asbestos.

As a result, he was diagnosed with asbestosis and ended up in a hospice facility in December of 2016.

Ironically, Michele was writing a book at the time. She explained,

Dad always wanted me to write. He was my biggest cheerleader while writing the book. It was very important to me to get the book done while he was still with us. I promised him I would have it done before he left us. Since my book is about messages from loved ones who passed, my father often asked me about spirit communication.

Michele's father knew he wouldn't be with her much longer. He told Michele, "Always listen for me. I will make every attempt possible to communicate with you."

In January, his illness had progressed, and he was terminal. They transported him to Middlesex Hospital, in Middletown, Connecticut.

The night before her father passed, he became almost completely unresponsive. Michele and her sisters were called to the hospital. Along with her sisters Debbie and Danette, they all held their father's hands and tried to comfort him as much as possible.

Breathing was difficult for him, and therefore speaking was too. But he still managed to speak his last words: "You're going to listen for me, right?"

Michele's father passed away the next morning on February 1. Michele explained,

I have an old flip phone that's at least ten years old that I kept in the second drawer in my bedroom bureau. It hasn't been plugged in and hasn't been used in a long time. Two days after Dad passed, I heard a buzzing sound. I couldn't determine where it was coming from! I searched and realize it was originating from the drawer in the bedroom. I opened the drawer and beneath some jewelry and small boxes was the flip phone. It was lit up and buzzing just like when I would get a phone call. I really didn't put two and two together and just figured it was somehow malfunctioning. I flipped the phone open and it stopped. I flipped it closed again and placed it on the bed.

That night, Michele was in bed talking to a friend from overseas on her current cell phone. Static started coming through the phone. She thought it was just a bad signal.

"Then the phone totally froze up! I couldn't hit any buttons. All of my apps started closing at once," Michele relayed.

She was in the process of restarting her phone, hoping it would reset itself. At the same time, the flip phone that was abandoned at the foot of her bed started buzzing and buzzing and lighting up.

She flipped open the phone, put her ear to the phone, and heard her dad's voice say, "Nett." This was followed by hearing difficulty breathing. Then she heard her name.

Halloween 2016, the phone rang and lit up once more. She answered it and it was her dad again, this time saying, "Michele."

Postscript: Michele's book was published January 3, 2017, less than a month before her dad passed away. They kept their promises. The book was finished, and her dad made contact.

CHARACTERISTICS

MESSAGE TYPE: OLD FLIP CELL PHONE, SMARTPHONE (INTERFERENCE)

FREQUENCY: TWICE

OTHER PHENOMENA: NO

FROM: DAD

WITNESSES: NO

ELEMENTS: SAYING HELLO? INTERFERENCE WITH SMARTPHONE WHEN CALLING ON AN OLD FLIP PHONE.

It Came from the Top of the Stairs
Lisa Mecham
Vernal, Utah, 1990

In August of 1990, Lisa's brother Joey passed away at a young age. After a period of mourning, the family moved all his belongings to the upper part of an addition on the house.

Joey preferred staying upstairs and often sat on the top stairs. After his death, the family still felt his presence at the top of the stairs in his usual spot. The family had a little dog named Baby, and Joey was the dog's favorite. Baby even had a special prance that he would do only when Joey was calling or talking to him.

One day, Baby was doing his special prance at the top of the stairs. Lisa's mom thought this might be a good opportunity to record at that spot and see if they could catch anything. Lisa explains,

We pressed record and planned on listening to it later. We wanted to leave the house to be sure if we captured anything, there would be no confusion over whether we made the sounds. When we listened back to the tape, you can hear us walk downstairs. You can hear the garage door opening and our car immediately leave. After that, there was activity. We heard someone speaking, but it was too soft and therefore indistinguishable. The voice sounded like it was almost pleading with us, but we just couldn't understand what was being said.

It's important to mention that Joey was learning to play bass. His bass guitar and amplifier were stored upstairs with his other belongings. His favorite song was "Crazy Train" by Ozzy Osbourne.

Getting frustrated at not being able to understand the voice on the tape, they all listened closely to hear what was next.

Lisa described the defining moment:

> There was a period of silence on the tape and then they heard the all-too-familiar bass line that Joey often practiced: The beginning part to the song. Only it wasn't the bass part on the recording; it was *Joey* practicing the bass part!

That was the moment that turned the family into believers. Together at once, the family all had the same thought: Joey was trying in multiple ways to prove it was him.

Fast forward to when some close friends of the family bought that same house. They loved Joey and had no fear about the events experienced there.

Lisa relayed the news from them with excitement:

> They told us that a TV upstairs in Joey's old room turned itself on and off at odd random intervals. As they investigated how the TV turned on, a few family members heard an unmistakable voice say "Joey" from within the TV! I still have that tape in storage somewhere and will share it if I can find it.

CHARACTERISTICS

MESSAGE TYPE: TELEVISION, RECORDING EQUIPMENT (VOICE, BASS GUITAR)

FREQUENCY: MULTIPLE

OTHER PHENOMENA: YES (BABY'S BEHAVIOR, VOICES, MUSIC, TELEVISION TURNING ON AND OFF AND PRODUCING VOICES)

FROM: BROTHER (JOEY)

WITNESSES: YES (FAMILY AND NEW FAMILY THAT MOVED IN AFTERWARD)

ELEMENTS: SAYING HELLO.

Netherworld Calling the Netherlands
Gretel Kuiper
Groningen, Netherlands, 2011

As a child, Gretel and her mom, Grietje, often discussed the paranormal, especially ghosts and the afterlife. They both shared a passion for those subjects. Since Gretel was a little girl, her mother always told her that when she dies, she will try to send a signal so Gretel would know there is life after death.

Gretel's mom passed away on January 6, 2011. As time passed, Gretel did not forget the pact. She kept looking for a sign of contact, but she saw nothing.

About two years later, Gretel felt a little push in the back of her shoulder; no one was there. She brushed it off when it happened, but made a mental note to pay attention in case the weird push occurred a few more times. She wasn't convinced, but it did cross her mind that maybe—just maybe—it was her mom. Gretel explains,

> I guess since I wasn't convinced, Mom turned it up a notch. One day, my husband, myself, and my son were home relaxing in the living room together. The television was off. I told my husband and son about the incident, but they were skeptical. Then I heard my name being called. "Gretel? Gretel?" I asked my skeptical witnesses

if they heard the voice too. They both nodded and agreed that they heard my mother's voice calling out, emanating from the television just as I heard it.

The television sat plugged in and off. Not long after this incident, Gretel was cleaning the living room. While dusting a table with a radio on it, she heard her mother's voice again. This time, it was coming right though the radio's speaker!

"Gretel? Gretel?" the voice once again called out.

"I haven't heard her call my name lately. Hopefully, she is at peace knowing that she helped solve the mystery we always were wondering about," Gretel told us.

CHARACTERISTICS

MESSAGE TYPE: TELEVISION, RADIO

FREQUENCY: MULTIPLE

OTHER PHENOMENA: NO

FROM: MOM

WITNESSES: YES (THE SON AND HUSBAND)

ELEMENTS: SAYING HELLO, KEEPING A PROMISE.

Our Song Plays at 10:30
Magen Hart
Columbia, Missouri, 2011

My grandmother Bessie passed away at 10:30 in the morning on January 7, 2011 (the time gains importance later in the story). She was like a second mom to me. Knowing she was sick, we would sit together and listen to the song "Holes in the Floor of Heaven" by Steve Wariner over and over again. The song is about a grandmother passing away.

Two days after her death, the radio turned itself on. I'm serious. It turned on of its own accord. And the time? 10:30 a.m.: the exact time of her death. It played our song! Throughout the next two weeks, when I had the radio on, that song would come on the radio at the same time of death: 10:30 a.m.

We have an old cordless disconnected phone that we kept plugged in to save Grandma's last voice mail messages to me. To play the messages back, you must press the button. Not with Grandma! Several times, her voice messages would start playing by themselves. No one was near the phone or touched the phone. Nevertheless, we unexpectedly heard her voice at odd moments.

We would hear, "Magen, this is Grandma." "Magen, call me." "Magen, this is Grandma, I'll call you back."

Those are a few of the messages that would start playing out loud without warning. I immediately started looking in the direction of the voice, expecting to see her there.

Author's note: We heard the messages. She is a sweet old lady with a Southern accent.

CHARACTERISTICS

MESSAGE TYPE: RADIO, ANSWERING MACHINE

FREQUENCY: MULTIPLE

OTHER PHENOMENA: NO

FROM: GRANDMA

WITNESSES: YES (OTHER FAMILY MEMBERS)

ELEMENTS: SAYING HELLO, FULFILLING A PACT TO LOOK OVER HER.

Calls from Deleted Cell Number
Alise Emerson
Northford, Connecticut, 2015

Alise's mom, Elois, passed away two days after Thanksgiving Day of 2009. Two years ago, what she thought was a typical call to her cell phone turned out to be something unexpected and impossible.

The number showed up as "Mom." Alise felt that was strange for two reasons: The first (and most obvious one) was that Elois was dead. The second reason was because Alise had deleted that phone number from her cell phone years ago. She kept it in her contacts for a while, but after several unpleasant views, she finally deleted it. How is this deleted number now contacting her? The biggest questions running through Alise's mind were: Who was on the other end of that line? Who would she hear? Alise was also just thinking about her and having one of those conversations you have with lost loved ones.

The moment of truth was upon her. She slowly and methodically answered the call. All she heard was static. She thought there was a possibility of there being a voice behind all the static, but Alise was careful not to conclude anything. It was hard to tell for certain.

What follows next is startling.

She remembers her mom telling the family about strange phone calls she was receiving. These repeated calls came in to her landline phone during the last few days of her life. The mother's calls were all static too. Eloise told Alise adamantly, "It was Dad." (Alise's dad died in 1990.)

Her mom said, "Dad's calling me," referring to her husband, Joseph.

"This is what convinces me it was my mom calling—just like Dad did," Alise told us.

CHARACTERISTICS

MESSAGE TYPE: CELL PHONE, LANDLINE PHONE

FREQUENCY: MULTIPLE

OTHER PHENOMENA: NO (BUT DUPLICATE PHENOMENA IN THIS MANNER IS RARE)

FROM: MOM, DAD

WITNESSES: YES (FAMILY MEMBERS)

ELEMENTS: SAYING HELLO.

Season's Greetings by HAM Radio
MJ Carcuro
Schenectady, New York, 2015

MJ's father, Clifford, passed away in December of 2014.

A year later, when searching in the attic for Christmas decorations, some of her father's old treasures caught her attention. There sat his old Hallicrafters HAM radio. It was a silver one from the 1960s. These were used by amateur radio operators to communicate with other local users. There was also a repeater feature that enabled you to talk to operators around the world.

MJ thought the radio was neat and set off to experiment. When she first plugged it in, nothing happened, so she assumed it was broken. Then she remembered that it used tubes to operate and they needed time to warm up. After a bit, she heard the familiar hum and saw the radio's lights glow.

MJ shared, "I heard nothing at all, but left it on while going about my business. About twenty minutes later, static began coming through. I went to the radio to see what it was doing. I heard my dad's voice call me by my childhood nickname."

"Hi, Pumpkin!"

MJ couldn't wrap her head around what just happened. She called her husband to see if it would happen again, so he could hear it too.

And he did. MJ says, "Soon after, static was heard, and then the un-mistakable exact voice of my dad saying 'Hi, Pumpkin!' Then she thought: Why not ask him a question?

MJ: Are you okay?

Dad: Yes.

MJ: Are you with Mom? (She passed away years before her father).

Dad: Yes.

Static followed, then silence.

"It was so comforting to know that Dad and Mom are okay and to-gether again!" MJ says.

CHARACTERISTICS

MESSAGE TYPE: HAM RADIO

FREQUENCY: MULTIPLE

OTHER PHENOMENA: NO

FROM: DAD

WITNESSES: YES (HUSBAND)

ELEMENTS: SAYING HELLO. DID SHE INTERRUPT HIM WHILE HE WAS USING HIS HAM RADIO?

Crossing Over Waycross by Phone
Lori Wanzo
Waycross, Georgia, 2010

In 2010, Lori's brother Johnny died from cancer at age sixty-seven. During his final days, he stayed at their mother's home. Lori explains,

I called Mom's house two days later to inquire about his funeral arrangements. I was using a landline phone to call Mom. I dialed her number and there was an odd waiting period before the phone started ringing. Before that, there was a lot of static. Then a man's voice came through.

It clearly said "Lori Ann." The voice was clearly my brother. After he spoke, the phone connected the call and started to ring.

Her mother answered that call and found a confused daughter on the line. Lori asked her if anyone was at the house that could have answered the phone before she did, but the only two people in the house were her mom and sister.

Lori explains, "This has never happened to me before or since. I believe this was my brother Johnny saying his last goodbye."

Characteristics

Message Type: Landline phone

Frequency: Once

Other Phenomena: No

From: Brother (Johnny)

Witnesses: No

Elements: Saying goodbye.

Confused Spirit of Munster
Amy Cak
Munster, Indiana, 2012

On December 31, 2011, Amy's husband, Phil, lost his mother. They stayed at his stepdad's house to help with things, including the funeral arrangements. Having trouble with sleep, they stayed up late watching TV. The phone rang, and on the other end was an old-sounding woman who was very upset and confused.

She asked, "Where is Tom?" (Tom is the stepdad's name.)

Tom got on the phone while the others listened in on the other line.

This lady kept pleading, "Tom! Where are you? Why did you leave me here? Why didn't you pick me up?"

Whenever Tom would ask the voice who she was, she would start in again, "Why did you leave me here? Why did you not pick me up?"

Then she hung up. Phil was losing the color in his face. His hair stood on end. The stepfather's complexion looked even whiter. Amy asked what happened.

Phil replied instantly, "I swear that was Grandma Eleanor!"

Eleanor was Tom's mom, but she died back in the 1990s. He distinctly heard her same thick Polish accent. He anxiously called the number back and the call originated from the same nursing home where she spent her final days. It's also the same place where she died.

CHARACTERISTICS

MESSAGE TYPE: LANDLINE PHONE

FREQUENCY: MULTIPLE

OTHER PHENOMENA: NO

FROM: MOTHER (ELEANOR)

WITNESSES: YES (HUSBAND, STEPFATHER)

ELEMENTS: SHE STILL WANTS TO GET OUT OF THE NURSING HOME?

Quarter Collector from Elsewhere
Mike Zoiss, paranormal investigator
Cincinatti, Ohio, 2007

Joanne's husband, Rich, passed away right before Christmas. They were out bowling when he had a sudden heart attack and died. He was collecting state quarters, and prior to his death, he only had two more to go to complete his collection.

When Christmas came, Joanne and her daughters were in the front room of their small house where the tree was set up. They were talking about Rich/Dad. During their heartbroken discussion of memories, two quarters rolled out from under the tree. It was the last two state quarters he needed to complete the collection! They knew it was from him.

Following this bizarre incident, the family would find quarters everywhere they went. They would appear in the most unusual places, such as falling to the ground when a gas hose was lifted at the pump. Another example was during the morning coffee and cigarette routine. As a coffee cup was lifted to take a sip, a quarter would be found underneath the cup. Quarters were even found under the wrapper of cigarette packs and between the sheets of a made-up bed, and they began appearing in midair with an audience. A small flash of light was followed by the familiar chink of a small metal object hitting the floor. The witnesses and recipients of these quarters are not limited to the immediate family. Joanne's daughter

Shelly had her boyfriend over one evening, and he felt something in the chest pocket of his shirt. He reached in the pocket and pulled out a quarter. When these quarters materialized, they were ice cold, which makes them obvious because a regular quarter in any pocket would be warmed by the body heat of the individual.

A significant "sign" was when Joanne found a line of quarters that stretched from within her bedroom to outside the door. Quarters were also found under her and the daughters' pillows. All of these quarters that appeared throughout a few years added up to more than 200. This unique collection is kept locked in the curio cabinet with other memories of her husband.

In addition to the quarters, there were weird phone calls, which the family started recording. Joanne would answer the phone and couldn't understand the caller's words. Instead, she heard grunting noises with syllables. The voice was hard to identify, but the laugh was not. It was unmistakably Rich's laugh.

Mike Zoiss was part of the paranormal investigator team called by the family for help in the case because there was other bizarre activity in the home. One of the group's members was sensitive to phenomena. He arrived at Joanne's home and met Shannon, Joanne's daughter; they said hello and shook hands. He knew Shannon had abilities to feel these things too and asked why she was resisting it. Shannon also received phone calls.

A voice said, "Why did you call me?"

Shannon said, "Say I love you, Shannon."

Shannon couldn't hear any of the conversation of the phone call, but Joanne could. The group, which included Bill and Jimmy, heard several of the recordings of the mysterious phone calls. The cadence of mimicking "I love you, Shannon" is heard.

Not all calls were friendly, however. Another entity threatened different family members and members of the group investigating. They tried to get video, but were unable to obtain any additional evidence. Activity in the house would come and go in cycles, so the group ran a recorder but did not ask any questions.

One member of the investigating group knew a pastor who was going to perform an exorcism on a woman in Colorado. Mike and a fellow investigator tagged along to check it out. Mike recorded it on a camcorder.

During the exorcism, the woman spoke what sounded like a foreign language. It was supposedly ancient Hebrew, but the woman only had what seemed like a fifth-grade education.

The woman looked at Mike and said, "I'm going to kill you!"

Afterward, Mike turned in for bed around 2:30 a.m., when Joanne called. In the background of the call was yelling and screaming so loud it hurt his ears. It was not the family, but some entity. In addition to the screaming sounds on the line, items were being thrown around the house by an invisible force. Mike told her they couldn't help because they were away in Indiana with the priest.

When Joanne called again, Mike's fellow investigator heard a little girl on the line and started talking to her. He thought it was her granddaughter. Then Joanne would come on the line. No one else was in the house. The strange little girl was not her granddaughter. Could Mike have been followed by the other phantom messages?

CHARACTERISTICS

MESSAGE TYPE: LANDLINE PHONES

FREQUENCY: MULTIPLE

OTHER PHENOMENA: YES (QUARTERS APPEARING, THREATENING CALLS)

FROM: HUSBAND (RICH), UNKNOWN ENTITY

WITNESSES: YES (FAMILY AND INVESTIGATORS)

ELEMENTS: QUARTER COLLECTION TIE-IN WITH PHONE CALL WITH RICH'S LAUGH.

4

A Few Celebrity Encounters

*The thing under my bed waiting to grab my ankle isn't real. I know
that, and I also know that if I'm careful to keep my foot under the
covers, it will never be able to grab my ankle.*
—Stephen King, *Night Shift*

The bizarre can reach anyone, anywhere. This includes celebrity actors,
authors, and musicians. Here are a few phantom visits of the celebrity kind.

Michael Moon
Metropolitan State Mental Hospital
Norwalk, California, 2004

Michael Moon is a Los Angeles–based actor
who has appeared in dozens of plays around the
United States and Sweden, and has appeared
in feature films such as *Horror 101, Horror
102, Day of the Dead 2,* and many others. He
is the president of Demon Theater, a company
dedicated to translating and staging the lesser-
known works of Ingmar Bergman.

Courtesy of Michael Moon.

The History of Metropolitan State Mental Hospital

Over 100 years ago when the Metropolitan State Mental Hospital opened its doors, it was self-sufficient due to a prosperous operating farm. Patients worked in the farm that produced all the food for the staff and patients. The buildings in the complex seem to make up a town of their own. Mental hospitals struggled with overcrowding, which made living quarters problematic and inhumane. Once scientists introduced psychotropic medications, treatment centers returned to a manageable occupancy.

Metropolitan State was accused of many patient abuses, which overcrowding might have motivated. Even today, assaults regularly occur, including one alleged murder. This time it's not the patients being abused; the staff is being attacked and overpowered by extremely psychotic patients. Either way, the place has a solid reputation for being haunted.

Michael's Experience

The hospital has been shut down for years and has been used as a movie set before. It consists of one large building and several smaller outer buildings. The building where we were filming looked like some kind of dormitory that slept about fifty patients with a caged-in office for the nurse on duty. There were also solitary confinement cells, which added to its creepy charm.

During the eight-day shoot, I and others noticed some weird phenomena happening. For example, in an abandoned building adjacent to the shoot, there was one particular light bulb on the ceiling that would turn on at exactly 6:10 each evening even though there is no power in that building and no wires connected to this light. I walked down the hallway and got extremely cold in one spot; I was jolted. I couldn't move. There was an AC vent above me and I thought it might be that, but I knew it wasn't. (That vent will become important in a bit.) We also had many unexplained problems with equipment, such as cameras, lights, and other electronics.

In the hallway, a voice would call your name, but when you went to look, no one was there. While filming, there were voices behind me: a man with a real low voice, then a young woman crying, a slap, then crying, then laughing. No one called cut! Where the noise was coming from, there was a long-forgotten chair used to tie and hold patients until a room could be arranged.

My wife, who was also in the movie, walked by that area and she heard someone say, "Sexy." I figured it was someone on the set. Again, no one was there.

When editing, they found voices on the film that were never heard when filming and did not originate from any of the actors. In one scene with two actors, one says a line, then there is a break, and then another line is spoken. There was a weird sound between their lines. The sound was isolated, and the volume was jacked up. The director/producer heard a female child's voice say, "Mom?" She also received a phone call one evening from an unknown number that said "Mom?" in the exact same voice and then hung up!

I heard footsteps coming up from behind and saw a shadow coming over me. I turned to look at it and it was gone. With all these audio interferences, we had to reshoot scenes frequently.

When a security guard noticed I became shaken up, he said that a lot of things go on in here.

He then warned me, "If you see the guy that's smoking and pushing an IV, look away and ignore him. He's bad news."

I asked him about the rust-colored stains in one of the rooms and was told that one of the doctors was allegedly molesting a female patient. The administration and the police worked together on the investigation. The police had him cornered in the room but before the police could break in, the doctor smashed her skull against a steam pipe next to a boiler and she died. The police broke in and shot him, but it was too late to save the woman. What was left were the bloodstains.

The guard also told me about the air conditioner that had not been working for four days during squelching hot weather. About two or three weeks prior, two patients went missing. When the air conditioning got fixed, a smell was coming through the vents. The repairmen discovered the two missing patients in the duct with a bed sheet wrapped around both of their necks. It appeared as though they tied the sheet to both of their necks and went in opposite directions killing both inside the crawl space. That was the very same spot that the cold jolted through me!

The director told me that the spirits seemed to be attracted to me. She recommended I say goodnight to them when I leave and thank them for letting me be there. That way, whatever was there would not follow me home. I thought that was ridiculous to say goodnight to spirits.

When we left at 2 a.m., we discovered the car wouldn't start. I complained out loud, "Can you please just let us go home?"

After asking, I was surprised to be able to start the car right away.

After arriving home, the unusual weirdness continued. There was tapping in the kitchen and noises in the bedroom. Pleading for silence, the "whatever(s)" complied.

Next, we set up the coffee maker for the next day. While busy getting things ready so we could be on the set at 6:30 a.m. the next day, my wife noticed something strange.

She asked me, "Why did you turn on the computer?"

The green light was clearly on and the computer booted up. We watched in horror as the cursor moved over to the icon to connect to the internet! It loaded a page on spirit photography that neither of us have ever visited before.

Feeling as if we've seen it all, the thought occurred to try the polite approach that the director suggested. We both said goodnight to the ghostly intruder. The computer window then closed and all by itself the computer turned off.

Even daytime shoots by different crews reported items being messed with and other phenomena. (Jimmy and Bill want to go there.)

CHARACTERISTICS

MESSAGE TYPE: FILM (VOICES CAPTURED), COMPUTER (TURNING ON, CONNECTING TO THE INTERNET, AND LOADING A PAGE ON SPIRIT PHOTOGRAPHY)

FREQUENCY: ONCE

OTHER PHENOMENA: YES (HAUNTING)

FROM: UNKNOWN ENTITY

WITNESSES: YES (OTHER ACTORS, EMPLOYEES)

ELEMENTS: COMPUTER MANIPULATION.

Ida Lupino
1942

Ida Lupino was an actor and the only one ever to star in and direct an episode of *The Twilight Zone* ("The Sixteen-Millimeter Shrine"). Her parents were London stage performers. Ida's grandmother often took care of her while her parents were away performing.

One night when Ida was a child, the phone rang at her grandmother's house where she was staying. Ida answered the phone and heard her father's friend Andrew on the line.

He said in a monotone emotionless voice, "Stanley? I must speak with Stanley. It's very important."

Ida said hello to Uncle Andy, as she called him, and explained that her parents were out performing.

Andrew repeated, "I need to speak with Stanley."

Ida relayed the message to her grandmother, who was confused by what Ida was telling her, so she grabbed the phone and listened to Andrew repeat his request.

She asked, "Andrew, are you ill?"

Instead of Andrew answering, the line went dead. She called the operator to ask what number just called, and the operator said no calls were made to her number in more than an hour!

That night, Ida was allowed to stay awake until her parents came home. Her grandmother told them about the call they received and the request Andrew made. Connie, Ida's mother, had to sit down. She looked like she was going to pass out. Her father turned pale and said that Andrew could never have called.

The grandmother insisted that he did call and thought they should call him back since he didn't sound like he was well.

Finally, her father said, "Mom, Andrew is dead. He hanged himself three days ago."

CHARACTERISTICS

MESSAGE TYPE: LANDLINE PHONE

FREQUENCY: ONCE

OTHER PHENOMENA: NO

FROM: ANDREW

WITNESSES: YES (GRANDMOTHER)

ELEMENTS: NO CALLS REGISTERED DURING THE TIME CONTACT WAS MADE. CALLS MADE RIGHT WHEN DEATH OCCURS.

Dean Koontz
1988

When Katherine Ramsland interviewed Dean Koontz for a biography about his life and work, he told many intriguing stories. One of them was a story about a phantom message.

On September 20, 1988, Dean had an experience he would not write about for nearly a decade, but he claimed it in his essay for *Beautiful Death* as his one possible encounter with evidence for life after death.

He was at work that day in his office when the phone rang. He picked it up and heard a female voice that sounded far away. She spoke with a sense of great urgency.

"Please, be careful!" she said.

A bit startled, Dean asked, "Who is this?"

He received no response. The woman repeated the warning three more times, and each time she said it, her voice became more distant.

When the line went silent, Dean sat there listening for a while, uncertain what to make of it. The voice sounded eerily like his mother, but she died nearly two decades ago.

"A voice is much harder to remember than a face," he said, "so I thought I was being melodramatic."

Since his number was unlisted, he concluded it was not a prank call aimed at him. Did someone simply dial a wrong number? Intrigued, he mentioned the incident to his wife, but told no one else.

It was such a strange call. I don't claim that it was a ghost. I don't know what I believe. It certainly was odd. People report these kinds of events all the time, and it's always struck me as interesting that everyone seems to have had an experience or two of the uncanny. Sometimes I believe that call was from my mother and sometimes that it was a very strange, serendipitous wrong number. I think you always have to keep some skepticism about things like this, but it's comforting to think that there may be a realm where the personality survives.

Two days following the haunting call, Dean visited his father, Ray, at the facility where he lived. The staff was dealing with Ray's behavioral problems, and they had asked Dean to come in to talk with him. Ray had punched another resident, a man with a walker, and the nurses were worried.

Dean was unaware Ray used some of his small allowance to go buy a yellow-handled fishing knife and had honed it to razor sharpness and oiled the hinge to make it open like a switchblade.

When Dean came into the room, Ray moved fast. He grabbed the knife from a drawer, and Dean had to try to wrestle it away from him. He just managed to avoid being slashed.

There were many witnesses to this altercation, and one of them called the police. Finally, Dean got the knife without incident and carried it out into the hall—just as the police arrived.

They drew their guns and ordered him, "Drop the knife!"

Dean was startled. "It's not me you want," he insisted. "It's him in there." He pointed into his father's room.

"Drop the knife!" they repeated, still pointing their weapons at him. Dean froze.

"All of a sudden," he recalls, "I realized that they were going to shoot me if I didn't drop the knife. They thought I was the perpetrator. So I dropped it and obeyed them. That was one of the worst moments of my life. My own stupidity almost got me killed."

Koontz later included this scene in his 1993 novel *Mr. Murder*, when Marty Stillwater, the protagonist, has a similar encounter (though under different circumstances) with the police.

Luckily, the police realized that Ray was the dangerous party. They took him to a psychiatric ward where he could be kept for observation.

But Dean thought again about the mysterious phone call. It had made him more vigilant, and as a result, had possibly saved his life. He never again received another such call.

CHARACTERISTICS

MESSAGE TYPE: LANDLINE PHONE

FREQUENCY: ONCE

OTHER PHENOMENA: NO

FROM: MOM? WRONG NUMBER?

WITNESSES: NO

ELEMENTS: WARNING CALL ABOUT DEAN'S FUTURE ALTERCATION.

Jennifer Runyon Corman
Orange County, California, 2012

Courtesy of Jennifer Runyon Corman.

Jennifer Runyon is an actress and producer known for her roles in *Ghostbusters, Another World, Up the Creek, Carnosaur,* and as Cindy Brady in the made-for-TV movie *A Very Brady Christmas.* She is also the co-host of *The Haunted Chronicles* radio show.

Jennifer's Experience

In 2010, our family moved into a new home. My son and daughter, along with my husband, all began to settle into our new place.

A FEW CELEBRITY ENCOUNTERS

On April 8, 2012, at about 10 a.m., I settled onto the couch in our family/media room to watch a movie. I heard a muffled conversation that was loud enough to be heard over the sound of the television. It was definitely a voice or set of voices, but the words were undecipherable. Thinking it might be the neighbors, I looked outside. No one was there. Settling back to return to the movie, the voices were heard again. Next, I turned the volume all the way down on the TV. There was silence. Within a few moments, however, one male voice was talking. Without explanation, I called my daughter to the room and told her to sit right where I was and listen. About twenty seconds later, the voice started again. It was a male voice for certain.

We realized that the voice was coming from the speakers on the ceiling. Those speakers were not connected to anything! My daughter stepped up on the couch to get a closer listen. She heard the voices but couldn't make out the words. I called my husband and let him listen. His opinion was that there must be a logical explanation.

I thought to myself that I must capture this on video. My iPad was readied and three different voices were recorded. One video in particular recorded the voices slightly clearer than the others. After following this phenomenon, it eventually went away and never occurred again.

About six months later, a crew came over to film as part of a *Ghostbusters* documentary. They asked me, "Do you believe in the paranormal?"

I said yes.

"Do you have any stories?" they asked next.

I told them about the voices from the speakers that were not connected and the crew was eager to investigate. They went upstairs to see what was between the floor to see if any voices could have originated from there. Nothing was found.

About a year later, I was telling my friend Jimmy Petonito about the strange event. Jimmy wanted to see the videos. He used a sound editing program to boost the volume and remove some background noise. After cleaning the files, Jimmy returned the recordings to me.

"Corman is here," I heard on one recording.

"Corman is home!" I heard on another.

So much for some random interference being the answer!

CHARACTERISTICS

MESSAGE TYPE: SPEAKERS (DISCONNECTED)

FREQUENCY: MULTIPLE

OTHER PHENOMENA: NO

FROM: UNKNOWN ENTITY

WITNESSES: YES (IT WAS RECORDED)

ELEMENTS: PERSONALIZED VOICES CAME OVER DISCONNECTED SPEAKERS. RECORDING OF THE VOICES WAS SUCCESSFUL.

Sir Paul McCartney
1995

Sir Paul McCartney believes that John Lennon was present when they recorded the 1995 Beatles single *Free as a Bird*.

Ringo Starr, George Harrison, and McCartney spoke of constant electrical trouble with the recording. McCartney also believes John was there when recording the single's B-side.

He said, "We put one of those spoof backwards recordings on the end of the single for a laugh, to give all those Beatles nuts something to do. I think it was the line of a George Formby song. Then we were listening to the finished single in the studio one night, and it gets to the end, and it goes, 'zzzwrk nggggwaaahhh jooohn lennnnnon qwwwrk.' I swear to God. We were like, 'It's John. He likes it!'"

CHARACTERISTICS

MESSAGE TYPE: RECORDING EQUIPMENT (ELECTRONIC DISTURBANCES, ALTERED STUDIO VOICES)

FREQUENCY: ONCE

OTHER PHENOMENA: No

FROM: FRIEND (JOHN), COINCIDENCE, OR RANDOM NOISE?

WITNESSES: YES (THE THREE BEATLES AND STUDIO PERSONNEL)

ELEMENTS: ELECTRONIC INTERFERENCE AND VOICE FOUND ON PLAYBACK NOT HEARD IN THE RECORDING PROCESS.

Harry Houdini
Houdini's Pacts for After-Death Communications

I had compacts with a round dozen. Each one promised me faithfully to come back if it were possible. I have even gone so far as to create secret codes and handgrips. Sargent had a certain word he was to repeat to me; William Berol, the eminent mental expert, gave me the secret handshake a few hours before he died and did not regain consciousness after silently telling me that he remembered our compact; Atlanta Hall, niece of President Pierce, a woman ninety years of age, who had had seances with the greatest mediums that visited Boston, called for me just before her death, clasped my hand, and gave me our agreed-upon grip, which she was to give me through a medium. They have never come back to me! Does that prove anything? I have attended a number of seances since their death, the mediums have called for them, and when their spirit forms were supposed to appear not one of them could give me the proper signal. Would I have received it? I'll wager I would have.

There was love of some kind between each of these friends who are gone and myself. It is needless to point out the love of a mother and son; the love of a real friend; the love of a woman of ninety toward a man who held her dear; the love of a philosopher toward a man who respected his life study—they were all loves, each strong, each binding. If these persons, with all the love they bore in their heart for me and all the love I have in my heart for them, did not return, what about those who did not hold me close, who had no interest in me? Why should they come back and mine not?

His Code with His Wife Bess Houdini

After Houdini died on Halloween in 1926, his wife Beatrice (Bess) offered $10,000 to anyone who could receive an authentic message from him. Bess held a séance every Halloween for the next ten years in hope of real communication.

Arthur Ford (1896–1971) was a clairaudient who claimed he could get a message from Houdini using his secret prearranged code. He did successfully. The problem was that Bess had told a reporter for the *Brooklyn Eagle* in 1927 that Houdini had longed to hear from his mother and that any authentic message would include the word "forgive."

In January 1929, Ford was ready to crack the secret code. He claimed to have a message from Houdini. Unfortunately, the code had been published the previous year by Harold Kellock in his book *Houdini, His Life-Story* (Harcourt, Brace and Company, 1928). Ford later admitted he got the code beforehand and that it was a hoax.

Perhaps he will call or use other technology someday or perhaps it's just more complicated than everyone having the ability to send messages.

For about two years after Houdini's death, Bess found hidden gifts from Harry with notes. He evidently hid them in order to be sure that he could communicate with her even if he couldn't return after his death.

5

Time Slips

When you sit with a nice girl for two hours you think it's only a minute,
but when you sit on a hot stove for a minute you think it's two hours.
—Albert Einstein

Time presents interesting questions and answers. As Richard Muller wrote in his outstanding book *Now, The Physics of Time,* even the notion of "right now" is not a stable moment: The universal time that you learned about from your parents and teachers does not exist. Not only will you get different times depending on the reference frame you pick (ground, airplane, Earth, sun, or cosmos), but you'll also get different *rates* of time. That means that the time between two events, two ticks on your watch, is not universal but depends on which frame of reference you choose. Ride in an airplane, or in a satellite, and from this effect you will live longer— according to an Earth frame. But you will not *experience* more time. Time just runs slower when you are moving. Your clock runs slower, but so does your heartbeat and your thinking and your aging. So you won't notice. That's the amazing thing about relativity. It isn't just clocks that run slower; it's everything. That's why we say that it's the pace of time that changes.

Confused yet? You're not alone. Time is a complex subject. So many of us are confident we can travel in time. However, those who are confident do not understand the physics involved. That doesn't mean it's impossible; we might just find the key to time travel. In fact, going into the future seems probable, but there is no similar mechanism that we know of yet that will bring us back in time. We have to remind ourselves that it's more complex and troublesome than armchair confidence or wishful thinking will deliver. We're discussing these issues because we are about to embark on time slip phenomena. Or at least it appears that way now—whenever that is. . . .

In cases that scream "time slip," senders of messages often allude to some of our current theories of quantum physics and the multiverse, which we will discuss further in Chapter 9. Some intriguing communications stress the idea of "space-time" and "dimensions" or other popular wording to convey their current circumstance or that of another identical version of themselves existing somewhere else, that is, doppelgangers. Ideas such as these have been reported:

"You are in time, we are outside of time."

"We are on Earth, but we are in space."

These types of statements that occur in messages suggest the contact might be from a time different than our own. Instead of being from a "dead" person, they exist in a way yet unknown to us but theorized by physicists. In that respect, you can deem the entire phenomenon as time slips, however, we reserved this designation for the exciting variation during which people hear an actual event taking place or there is a unique experience of a message delivered from a different time. We call them "time slips" for the lack of a better identifying commonality. And also, because it's cool.

Call from the Future Predicts 9/11
David R. Fritz
Cape Cod, Massachusetts, 2001

It was one month before 9/11. David was working as an alcohol and drug addiction counselor in Cape Cod, Massachusetts.

David received a call on his cell phone that went straight to voice mail. He checked the message for a call-back number and time, but there was none.

David told us: "I listened to the message. While listening, I got this bad, eerie feeling of dread. It's hard to explain, but I felt sick instantly. There was no voice, but a lot of wind and the sound of crunching metal. In the background, you could hear a crowd of people screaming in terror."

He kept receiving these mysterious calls every morning. All of them lasted exactly three minutes. The calls were so puzzling that David played the messages to his girlfriend at the time and three of his close friends. He didn't tell them what he thought they would hear or feel. He just asked them to listen to the messages he received. Unanimously, everyone heard the same disaster scene and they too were filled with trepidation. One friend couldn't even bear to listen to the entire message.

These frightening calls from an unknown source prompted David to get rid of the cell phone and get a new phone, with a new carrier. The calls finally stopped, and mornings were once again uneventful.

All of that changed on the morning of September 10, 2001. David received one last call the morning before the towers came down. As usual, the call went right to voice mail. The same exact message was on his new phone! Soon David would discover that those sounds of metal and screams may have belonged to the terrorist strike the next day on September 11, 2001.

After 9/11 occurred, no other calls have been received. David, and all of us, may never know if they were hearing a disaster yet to come in our time. We do know that it resonated in David and the others who listened to it as an experience they will never be able to forget.

CHARACTERISTICS

MESSAGE MODE: CELL PHONE

FREQUENCY: MULTIPLE

OTHER PHENOMENA: NO

FROM: UNKNOWN ENTITY

WITNESSES: YES (DAVID, FRIENDS)

ELEMENTS: THE EVENT IS HEARD OVER THE PHONE INSTEAD OF HEARING A PERSON. DAVID SHARED THE MESSAGES WITH THREE FRIENDS AND GIRLFRIEND. MULTIPLE CALLS ARE MADE UNTIL THE EVENT TAKES PLACE. THEN THEY STOP AS IF TIME CAUGHT UP AND IS NOW SYNCHRONIZED WITH THE INCIDENT. THESE CALLS APPEAR TO HAVE ELEMENTS OF A WARNING CALL, BUT IT COULD BE A TIME SLIP THAT PERMEATES THE PARALLEL UNIVERSE AND DOES SO IN THE FACE OF DISASTER.

Emergency Call from the Past
Donna
Litchfield County, Connecticut, 1984

In the book, *The Haunted House Diaries: The True Story of a Quiet Connecticut Town in the Center of a Paranormal Mystery*, Donna, the mother of the family at the farmhouse located in a paranormal flap area, received a call during which a disaster was heard happening over the phone. This time, our event appears to be from the early 19th century. Donna's diary entry of the event follows.

Diary Entry 109 (Summer 1984)

I was home all alone. The phone rang, and I picked it up thinking it was just like any random call we get. I couldn't have been more wrong.

I answered and said "hello," and on the other end there was a commotion. It was as if I were listening to something happen in real time, but it sounded like it was from a past time by the Victrola-like voices and noise. Either that, or I thought it was some type of crank call.

After a few moments, it became very apparent that this was no crank call. It sounded like there was a real disaster in the making going on. There was a voice echoing in what sounded like the distance as he said, "Ahoy, matey! Freighter up ahead!" Then I heard men yelling in the background. There was confusion, splashing sounds as if people were abandoning ship, and other sounds typical of an old-time marine emergency. Then the line just went dead and I heard the dial tone. I know in my mind, my ears were witnessing a real incident from the past that somehow came through the phone.

CHARACTERISTICS

MESSAGE MODE: LANDLINE PHONE

FREQUENCY: ONCE

OTHER PHENOMENA: YES (FLAP AREA)

FROM: UNKNOWN ENTITY

Computer and Television Contact from Another Time
Adolf Homes
Rivenich, Germany, 1995

Being a paranormal instrumental transcommunication (ITC) investigator, Adolf Homes enlisted the help of a phone monitoring company for his experiments. He still received bizarre phone calls. In two months, his monitored line received four mysterious phone calls that were not shown on the monitoring service report as being made. The phenomena had only started, as he would soon see.

Adolf Homes reported that he received a strange message typed onto his computer screen from a deceased colleague named Frederick Jürgenson, who was a Swedish filmmaker and one of the pioneers of EVP. He was an eminent European artistic personality of his time. Holmes took his video camera and filmed the screen that had all German writing on it.

The German message translation is as follows:

Here Friedel from Sweden is making contact. ["Friedel" was the pet name the voices, his friends, and family used to call Frederick.] Dear Humans. As is known to you, we are in a position to enter into your structure at choice. I send you repeatedly a projection of myself but with your appearance (the appearance known to you). The time indication [on the video camera] is not correct for you. The projection is the quanta of no space-time since 17.1.1991.

Each [one] of your and our thoughts has its own electromagnetic reality that does not get lost outside of the time structure. Not only our so-called transcontacts, but the consciousness of the universal whole [as] purely mental/spiritual and in principle creates all physical and psychical forms. From this point of view, we too, are still humans. This collective undertaking creates all forms. These, in their turn, represent illusions, because they change. Many of us are in a position to adopt [a] physical shape. Please transmit my message to all men. This says to you F. Jürgenson.

An image of the message Adolf received on his computer. *Photo courtesy of Anabela Cardoso.*

Adolf's television turned itself on at the same time the message was received. On the TV was an image of Jürgenson that he referred to in the computer message as a "projection of myself with your appearance."

The image received is below and a duplicate photo of Frederick is on the right for comparison. He received many messages over the course of time from the puzzling messenger.

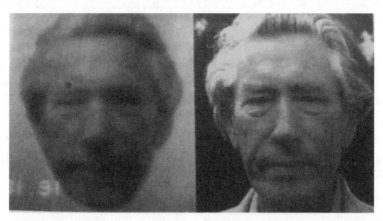

Left: The image of Frederick videotaped on Adolf's television screen in a different room than the computer. Right: A real-life photo of Frederick. *Photos courtesy of Anabela Cardoso.*

CHARACTERISTICS

MESSAGE MODE: COMPUTER, TELEVISION

FREQUENCY: MULTIPLE

OTHER PHENOMENA: No

FROM: STRANGER (ADOLF)

WITNESSES: No

ELEMENTS: FREDERICK'S WORDS, IF THEY ARE HIS, DESCRIBE THE HOLOGRAM MULTIVERSE THEORY.

Strange Letter Predicts Visitors
Donna
Litchfield County, Connecticut, 1979

Here is a letter experience discovered on the "Connecticut Skinwalker Ranch" as our beloved friend Paul Eno sometimes refers to it. This is also from the book *The Haunted House Diaries: The True Story of a Quiet Connecticut Town in the Center of a Paranormal Mystery.*

Diary Entry 89 (Spring 1979)

This is kind of a strange thing. Last week, Mom opened her mailbox by the front door, and there was a note in it from two old friends. It said, "Sorry we missed you—Betty and Fred." The only people she knows by that name are Betty and Fred Wilcox. She hadn't seen them in nearly thirty years, and said she'd have to locate their number and call them. She was clearly upset that she had missed them. The writing on the note was in pencil and very shaky. The pencil had been pressed down real hard onto the paper. When she called them, they were very surprised to hear from her. They said they had not stopped by and didn't leave a note. In fact, they have not been in the area for years.

Today she got a note from Ruby and Garnet. It was almost the same writing—sort of shaky and pressed deeply into the paper. She had not seen them in many years and commented that she would call them and have them over for lunch. That afternoon, they appeared at the door. Mom welcomed them in, and told them that she had gotten their note and was sorry that she had missed them. They looked at each other clearly puzzled, then looked at her and told her that they had not left a note. They hadn't stopped, and, in fact, had just decided to do so a few minutes before. They no longer live in the area, and it was an unplanned stop as they were just passing through.

CHARACTERISTICS

MESSAGE MODE: LETTERS

FREQUENCY: TWICE

OTHER PHENOMENA: YES (FLAP AREA)

FROM: UNKNOWN ENTITY

WITNESSES: YES (DONNA, MOTHER, RUBY, GARNET)

ELEMENTS: PREDICTION OF FUTURE EVENTS (OR PAST EVENTS FOR THEM).

My Boyfriend Heard Himself Die on the Phone
Cheryl Phillips
Charlevoix, Michigan, 2002

My boyfriend, Joe, was living in an apartment building that used to be the old Charlevoix Hospital and Nursing Home. It was haunted! There were many black shadow figures. There was a feet-shuffling entity that wheezed; it was heard in the other side of the basement by us, as well as visitors. I also heard people working in the coal furnace area that was located near our apartment. We also heard the elevator go up and down, but no one was ever there. It has been out of commission since the 1970s. There were also wailing sounds from the apartment above when no one was home; I went up there to check on them because I thought someone was hurt. The new tenant from upstairs would come running down to our unit all enraged. He claimed there were loud sounds coming from our apartment when, in fact, all was quiet. The manager had to finally confront him.

And there's more: An old disconnected phone in the pool room rang. One tenant woke up to a whole group of shadow figures. A new tenant ran out into the parking lot hysterical after she saw her closet hangers violently shaking. Door knocks and doorbell rings at our apartment door occurred when no one was there. And then, the weirdest part of the haunting happened: the phone call. The one we all knew was inherently different.

I was on my way to visit Joe at the apartment when he received the strange call. When I arrived, he was anxious to tell me what happened. He received a call that came from my landline phone, but no one could have made that call! And then what he told me next was disturbing and chilling. All he could hear was the loud sound of a respirator and a loud beating heart. It freaked him out! He let his roommate listen as well. Joe thought maybe one of us played an elaborate joke on him, although he knew that would be out of character for any of us to do. I assured him that no one from our house made that call. I even asked my young children about it. I already knew they didn't have the capacity to pull off such a prank, and had no motivation to do so. They really liked Joe. I know for a fact that none of us made that call.

About two months later, Joe died of a sudden massive heart attack at age 51. We were all in shock. My daughter saw a large floating orb glide across the living room soon after Joe died. I remember that hours before his death, I kept trying to reach him. I made thirteen calls to his sister. I just felt a strong urge to talk to him. Unfortunately, there was no answer.

CHARACTERISTICS

MESSAGE MODE: LANDLINE PHONE

FREQUENCY: ONCE

OTHER PHENOMENA: YES (HAUNTED APARTMENT BUILDING)

FROM: UNKNOWN ENTITY

WITNESSES: YES (CHERYL, BOYFRIEND, ROOMMATE)

ELEMENTS: HEARD A FUTURE EVENT, WARNING CALL, TIME SLIP.

Text Messages from Your Future Self
A fictional composite of a few of these rare cases, 2004

Imagine if you texted yourself but you didn't. Perhaps that can be written off to some electronic misfire that you are unaware of and don't pretend to understand. That's what recipients of this phenomena thought at first. These messages are different though. It is rare, but certainly not the first reported cases of receiving phantom messages from the future.

Here's a typical scenario: It was a typical night in 2004. A text message showed up on Jaime's phone. The message was blank. She looked where the phone number would be and was instantly confused. The area code number was recognized as familiar, but the other numbers were a mystery and certainly not from her phone's contact list.

She texted back, "Hey, who is this?".

A few minutes passed, and Jaime received a reply text from the same number. Blank again. Then she noticed the date and time of the message. The text was dated from the future! Ten years in the future, from the year 2014. The date was the exact month and day that her and her now husband met. This wasn't the type of special day that friends or family would know.

Struck with intrigue, Jaime put her detective thinking cap on and got to work on solving the mystery. Her first step was to call the mystery number. She received a not-in-service message. This was getting weirder. A text dated from the future that knows a date only she would know (even her husband often forgot it) texts her on a number that's not in service!

When her husband, Tom, got home from the office, she immediately checked with him. He confirmed he didn't text her. Then she sat him down and told him the story. Tom was looking at her skeptically until she showed him the strange blank text message with the future date. Now they both shared the puzzle.

The next day, the strange text was all Jaime could think about. She grabbed her cell phone upon waking and took a screen shot of the text. Then Jaime went back to work on the case.

She spent time Googling to see if anyone had experienced anything similar to this. She found tales of similar future phantom messages that appear on wedding anniversaries, at the time of death of a loved one, or other meaningful dates intertwined with the unexplainable contact.

Jaime started asking questions. Is this my future self trying to say hello by using a date in place of being able to send an actual text message? And if so, how? Is it the future me time traveling? That seems unlikely, given the short period in the future the text is from, if we believe that's the time when the actual message was sent. She was no closer to any solution, other than knowing there is not a simple one for this text. This message was not the norm. Jaime accepted that it was from her future self since the day in question was too obscure to be a hack or a practical joke. And why? By who?

Being the relentless sleuth, she occasionally dialed the number to try to make some sort of contact. After all, the number was the most solid lead she had. On one such attempt, she dialed the number and a young woman answered. Jaime was very excited! She had been trying a few times a year and finally someone picked up. She explained her predicament to the lady and it wasn't long before she was confused, bored, annoyed, or all three. Who could blame her? The story sounded too incredible even as Jaime heard herself retell it to the woman.

CHARACTERISTICS

MESSAGE MODE: TEXT (FROM CELL PHONE)

FREQUENCY: TWICE (INITIAL MESSAGE AND RETURN MESSAGE)

OTHER PHENOMENA: NO

FROM: FUTURE SELF

WITNESSES: YES (HUSBAND)

ELEMENTS: BLANK TEXT, DATED IN THE FUTURE, SAME DATE AS DAY THEY MET (COINCIDENCE OR SIGNAL?).

The Dodleston Messages Revisited
Ken Webster and Deb Oakes
Dodleston, England, 1984

I return to Guy Lyon Playfair, who concluded: "It may be that the wisest course to follow after obtaining positive evidence of any kind in any area of psychical research is to make use of it for personal enlightenment, and therefore to keep quiet about it!" Now, just over ten years after our own adventures, it sadly seems good advice. Meadow Cottage was important to us. It is sufficient.
—Ken Webster

One of the most captivating cases of phantom messages began in 1984 and lasted for sixteen months. Ken Webster and Deb Oakes documented the events during that time. They lived in the village of Dodleston, near the English border of Wales. We're going to highlight parts of the story and add new interview material never before released. This case boasts more than 300 phantom messages.

The story started when the young couple decided to renovate their small cottage. Nicola, a friend, was staying with them during her break from school. After they finished painting the kitchen, footprints were found in the fresh paint on the walls. Puzzled, Ken painted over it and went to bed. The next morning, new footprints were found in a different part of the kitchen. Often when they came home, items in the kitchen were stacked in a pyramid—cat food cans and Pepsi cans, for example. Ken's bandmate was the first suspect for these assumed pranks, but the mysterious stacking continued, and the couple quickly became annoyed. Other poltergeist activity included the house shaking, rearranged furniture, voices, items thrown, a bent and straightened copper pan handle, noises on the roof, items charred or burnt, and items appearing, disappearing, or changing location. Soon, their experiences were going to become bizarre beyond imagination.

Ken was a high school economics teacher, so he had access to the BBC microcomputers and sometimes borrowed them for different projects. He eventually brought one home with him, as he figured Nicola would find a computer useful for her schoolwork. It was a very early 8-bit, released in 1981. The software was Edward 2; it had a word processor and no graphics.

Upon returning home from his friend's house, Ken discovered a new file on the word processor entitled "KDM." The message was very strange and the formatting was all wrong. What was extra unusual was seeing that the message appeared to be in Old English and had capitalization and font abnormalities. Ken got the feeling you get while watching a horror movie: shivers. All he could focus on was the two first lines:

Ken Deb ni c True A re The NIGHTmares Of a pErson t hat FEARs…

When Ken read it, he thought it was a type of poem written in Old English. He printed the screen and took it to Peter Trinder, a fellow teacher at the high school. Peter was intrigued by the accuracy of the writing; it really did appear to be from the 16th century. Could this be genuine?

Peter decided to type out questions to "whomever it is" to see if more could be discovered about this mysterious messenger. It answered. The person lived in the reign of Queen Elizabeth II.

The next message asked a question: "Does everyone here have a horse?" Then he shared that the king was Henry the VIII and the date was March 28, 1521! The strange message then goes on to read:

I WRYTE ON BEHALTHE OF MANYE—WOT STRANGE WORDES THOU SPEKE THOU ART GOODLY MAN WHO HATH FANCIFUL WOMAN WHO DWEL IN MYNE HOME . . . WITH LYTES WHICHE DEVYLL MAKETH . . . 'TWAS A GREATE CRYME TO HATH BRIBED MYNE HUSE —L.W.

Modern English translation:

I write on behalf of many—What strange words you speak. You are a worthy (good) man who has a fanciful woman, and you live in my house with lights which the devil makes. It was a great crime to have stolen my house. —L.W.

Ken was told he was talking to Lukas Wainman, who lived in the 16th century, and who was a fellow of Brasenose College, Oxford University, and a resident of the same cottage. Lukas was well aware he was communicating with a couple living some 400 years in the future. In his time, he understandably feared being convicted of witchcraft. Sharing his fears, the following message was received:

WHEN THY BOYSTE DIDST COME THER WERT A VERS ON'T THAT SAID ME WERE NOT TO AXE OF YOUR UN-KYND KNOWINGS FOR THY LEEMS BOYSTE WILT BE NAMORE.

Modern English translation:

When your light box came with the writing on it, they told me I am not to talk to you or my light box will be no more. (He thought that Ken was the same person as someone else, but then learned Ken was from the year 1985.)

Lukas claimed to live in his own cottage on the same piece of land that Ken and Deb were currently on. He also said that the device (the computer) materialized in his cottage, and he read the questions and then answered. For Lukas, the computer messages were from the future whereas

The Dodleston Cottage. *Photo courtesy of Gary M. Rowe.*

his messages to Ken and Deb were from the past! They were living people communicating on this device, each in their own respective space-time.

Lukas's servant believed the device to be evil and the work of the devil. Lukas referred to it as "the box of lights."

They were fascinated, yet the couple remained highly skeptical. Ken, Deb, and Peter headed off to the library in search of the names and places Lukas mentioned. After finding the research to be tiring, they figured it would be easier to debunk it by catching the prankster entering and leaving messages. As they planned their trap, the messages kept coming. In one of them, Lukas said the equivalent of "I don't know why you're in my house, but you may stay as long as you like. I know you are real now."

They learned more about Lukas as he left messages such as "My servants can't see the light box," in old English. Ken and Deb were getting the picture that Lukas was having his cottage haunted too. Could this actually be a mutual "haunting"?

Ken continued to print out all the messages. He passed them on to Peter, who carefully examined and translated the messages using the Oxford English Dictionary as the primary language research source. Peter was convinced the messages were genuine from that period of time. If not, it was a hoax by an unusually educated and dedicated prankster. Fast and lengthy responses to unanticipated questions added to the implausibility that a prankster could have such a mastery of correct 16th-century language.

Ken tried to describe a car when replying to Lukas's inquiries about the use of horses in the future. To aid in understanding, he cut out a photo of a Jaguar and put it on the desk next to the computer. When he returned to check, the photo was gone and there was a reply! Lukas told them that without a horse, their so-called car would not go far! He also asked what kind of wood the image was made from. Deb was in the house while these messages were left.

When Ken walked over to the computer again, a photo was found back in the same area it was left. However, the photo was not the same. It was charred, aged, and lost all its color. The photo was obviously brittle. Ken was extremely careful so it wouldn't crumble in his hands. The conclusion was instant, yet uncanny: The photo came back aged and was now parchment. It couldn't be a hoax unless the prankster was able to falsely age the paper in a realistic manner and do it in record time. As if that were not difficult enough, the pranksters would have had to find a way to gain access to the cottage undetected and take the photo when first placed there, then enter once more and leave the exact same photo after aging it. That was all less likely than their strange conclusion.

Lukas also confided that the lady friend he was courting was upset with him for having another woman in the house! Moving on, he was back to desperately wanting to know more about our future world. His most pressing question was about the object (a folder) near the computer. He couldn't figure out what it was made of (it was plastic).

Over time, Ken and Deb incorporated Old English into their communications the best they could. Lukas also asks about curing sickness, the king's reign, and other logical inquiries.

Eventually, Ken confronted Lukas and said some of the information Lukas gave about himself was incorrect. Lukas confessed that he had not been using his real name because he was wary of who Ken and Deb were and didn't want to get too personal until he had an idea of who he was really talking to.

Lukas mentioned that Deb had visited him before. Deb confided that she had been having some strange vivid dreams during which she saw an unknown man walking through the cottage in old-fashioned clothes. They stood in silence when they found chalk writing on the wall that spelled out a name: Lukas.

Poltergeist activity occurred during the whole ordeal, including the computer ending up in the bathroom at one point. The scariest moment for Deb was when she felt a coldness and invisible "hands" pulling her hair. At times, they stayed away from the cottage to get a break from the poltergeist, the intense ongoing message drama, and the renovations.

A few weeks passed and then they got a message from someone who was allegedly from the future and who went by the name or title "2109." Lukas was also still in contact and finally shared his real information. His name was Tomas Harden. Their research uncovered that there was a record of him going to the college he mentioned for eight years and was then expelled. Also, he lived in the same cottage. His story checked out accurately with the records they found in the library using his real name.

Tomas explained that Deb showed up in his home, and he was mad. Deb's latest dream included seeing a woman in the living room with Tomas. He saw her, smiled, and introduced Deb to his lady friend, Kathryn. She looked back at him like he was crazy. Tomas and Kathryn then had a fight.

The next message didn't come from Tomas; it came from his friend. He said they brought ruin to Tomas. Word got out. Tomas was accused of witchcraft and was locked in the dungeon facing execution for heresy. Ken and Deb felt horrible. They typed that they felt very bad and wanted to help in any way they could.

Tomas's friend convinced the sheriff to go to the home to see the box of lights himself, and Ken and Deb received a message from the sheriff. He wondered if the object was physically in the house. He tried to move the box of lights, but it wasn't solid. The sheriff was an instant believer.

After a few exchanges, Ken typed, "We are not demons, but we have the power of demons. If you don't release him, we will make you burn in hell!"

It worked. Tomas was released under house arrest and thanked them dearly for saving his life. He was still worried about getting into trouble, because he couldn't help but work on writing a manuscript that detailed all of his experiences. Tomas was writing a book!

The computer messages moved to paper at times too. Charcoal and paper were left for Tomas and messages appeared by those means. Deb felt charcoal would be easier for him to write with since it was a familiar tool.

Tomas confided in the couple. He originally thought they were 2109, the friend who first brought and introduced the light box to him.

Ken was intrigued. He typed, "Calling 2109?"

He received a message back: "We are sorry."

They called Peter Trinder again for help because there was now chalk writing on the kitchen floor. Peter arrived and recognized the writing as Latin. The haunting continued as they returned to the house. Their heavy furniture was mysteriously piled up in the corner of the living room. Tomas also experienced the roof noises, causing us to wonder if he was victim to the same poltergeist.

The Society for Psychical Research (SPR) was contacted for help. They found the messages fascinating, especially the ones from the futuristic or alien entity known as 2109:

> Tomas is a person living in the 16th century, but unknown to him, he is not quite what he seems to be. This is a Tachyon universe, but it's hard for you to understand now. We shall answer as you wish it in terms of physics, then it shall be so, but remember that our limits are set by your abilities.

"Tachyon" refers to a particle theory first proposed in 1962 by O. M. P. Bilaniuk, V. K. Deshpande, and E. C. G. Sudarshan. They were originally called "metaparticles" and move faster than the speed of light. For these particles to exist and act that way, new rules of physics need to be invented just so this theory could work. This automatically weakens the validity of the proposal. If the theory relies on too many assumptions, the probability of it being true diminishes exponentially. In the future, the basics of it might be found to be true. But as of right now, there's no reason to believe it is.

In 2011, the discovery of a faster-than-light particle was reported, however, faulty equipment caused this inaccurate reading. To date, no evidence has been presented to support the existence of this fast-moving particle.

Tachyons, however, are very much alive in physics. Today, the term is used to describe a quantum field with an imaginary mass, rather than faster-than-light particles. These quantum fields have become significant in modern physics because of not being localized and because of their instability. The Higgs Boson is a Tachyon, so it's important!

We admit physics can be confusing, so the bottom line is: If 2109 is real and it is referring to a quantum field of imaginary mass, tachyons do have the potential to hold significant new knowledge in physics. No doubt in the years to come, we will hear more about how these fields fit into or expand the physics of tomorrow.

To validate that our future is known and that their past was known, SPR asked for the next date of the supernova; 2109 responded with the specific date and coordinates. Years later, the date and location allegedly turned out to be exact if you view the supernova from outside our galaxy!

The Society of Psychical Research typed ten questions on their own computer unseen by Ken, Deb, Peter—or anyone else—and guarded it awaiting answers. The original computer was examined. Nothing was found. We contacted SPR and verified that they did investigate Dodleston, yet no report was on file. (More on their involvement later.)

Since this was before the Internet, these early computers didn't have the processing ability to send or receive messages like we do today. Ken was disappointed; they still had no answers.

The entity 2109 gave Ken a phone number to call to explain about 2109. The phone number belonged to Gary Rowe, a ufologist and stranger to Ken. Gary understood the meaning of 2109 and came out to investigate; 2109 expressed the desire to communicate with Gary privately. Ken was asked to print the messages and deliver them without ever reading them.

Ken compiled the messages and put them into envelopes as instructed. Deb was shocked to discover strange symbols on the previously blank envelopes. Some envelopes even contained objects. Gary was completely skeptical at first, but now he knew this was genuine.

The entity 2109 provided a date that all communications between them would end. The date came and went, and a guest insisted they try again to communicate. Ken obliged, and a message did appear, but it wasn't Tomas. The message had no meaning to Ken or Deb. However, the guest turned white when she read the message and fainted. After recovering, she refused to talk about it with anyone.

By now, Ken and Tomas considered each other dear friends, and Ken missed him. He even described the night the computer showed up:

> There was a green light shimmering on the wall. From the light stepped what I thought was the devil himself. I was paralyzed with fear. It didn't talk like the devil though. It left me the box of lights. Kathryn couldn't see it. She began singing while the two were messaging and it was heard. The words she was singing showed up on the computer screen!

Ken and Debbie realized that Tomas may not have had to type anything on the computer when communicating.

The last day of communication arrived, and Tomas said:

> One day we will all sit down at my table for wine and meat by the river of Oxford and we will read each other's books; you should write a book about this and I will write a book about this. In your time, my book will be very old, but I shall not go to my god until it is written. And then we will all be truly embraced. My love to you all. I shall await for you in Oxford.

They also received a final message from 2109 saying Ken should write the book, as well as this: "As long as your kind cannot penetrate our world, we will be safe. Tomas did finish the book before he died and hid it in a secure place, and it shouldn't take long to find it. He wrote it in Latin with the help of a friend."

No one has been able to find this alleged hidden 400-year-old book.

Was the entity posing as different messengers? Ken mentioned there were multiple communicators involved, and he believed some were messing with them. In the end, he was uncertain as to what to make of it all. He did believe Tomas was who he said he was when he was the one leaving messages. Ken was angered by 2109's poor English and spelling, which added to the confusion surrounding its authenticity.

The cottage kitchen video set up. *Photo courtesy of Gary M. Rowe.*

John, a friend and later roommate, characterized Ken in this way: "Ken was a pretty serious type of person; he had a great sense of humor but was a fairly solitary and sensitive kind of guy, certainly not the type of person to leave himself open to public ridicule."

A most interesting way to interpret this case is to read what Tomas wrote (the modern English translation follows):

MYNE GOODLY FOOL MYNE LINKMAN THINKETH THAT THOU ART BE AL MYNE PAN H'SAYETH THAT ME MAKETH LYK DIVINSTRE BUT I KNOW YOW LYVE NOWE HE ALS SAYETH THAT MYNE BLOOD BE POYSOND AN THAT IT BE MYNE WEEK HIGNED FANCY BUT LUNE ME NAT METHENKE AN TOLDE HEM SO I ALS SEID 'TIS LYK FAIRYMGOLD AN THAT TO HOLD IT CLOSE TIL ME WRYTS BOOKE.

Modern English translation:

My pleasant fool, my servant, thinks that you are all in my head. He says I act like a seer but I know you live now. He also says that my blood is poisoned and that it is my weak-hinged imagination; but I am not mad, I think, and told him so. I also said it is like fairy gold [that he should] keep it secret until I write a book.

And then Tomas sums it up better than we can today: "METHYNK YOW ARN A HISTORIE BOKE THAT HATH ITS FRONTE AN BACK SKYN JOYNANT WE ARN EECHE A SYDE."

The modern English translation of this message reads: "I think we are a history book that has its front and back pages joined together. We are each a side of it."

Gary M. Rowe, DRad, FBIMS on Dodleston

Gary M. Rowe was born in Staffordshire in 1942. He is an international lecturer and longtime investigator of anomalous phenomena. Gary is the founder and director of the Forward to Aquarius paranormal and psychical research organization. He is also cofounder of the Welsh Federation of Independent Ufologists. Gary is married with one son and currently resides in Rhyl, North Wales.

Courtesy of Gary M. Rowe.

Gary's Experience

If this story had not been made public or turned into a book, I would never have spoken about it to another living soul. I sincerely wish it had not.

For me, the Dodleston messages are not a story or a book. Instead, it's a part of my life. One that has profoundly impacted everything I thought I knew. It changed me forever. The information gained came at a price. A high price. I wish I was at liberty to discuss my communication with 2109.

I am not a wealthy person. I believe the information I sit on could make me rich and famous. I believe I was selected due to knowing that I am a person who can be trusted to keep this secret sacred. The secret has its own built-in evidence.

My involvement:

One evening, I was sitting at home watching television with my wife. The phone rang. Someone I didn't know told me they had received a message to ring me. He began telling me about bizarre communications. It all sounded like nonsense to me. I was invited to meet them at Peter Trinder's house, and I decided to go.

There, the atmosphere was tense. They were convinced they had finally discovered who was behind these strange events. Me? I was equally convinced I was dealing with a bunch of hoaxers. I was certain that this was simply a wind-up. Some pranksters heard about my research into the weird and strange, and therefore assumed I must be gullible and easily fooled.

I've investigated a multitude of strange phenomena and pride myself on usually being able to get to the bottom of cases. I saw this as a challenge, determined to discover what was going on and ultimately expose the fraudsters. I considered this to be a useful exercise to test my investigative skills and to see how long it would take for me to solve it. Why not go along with it?

At Peter Trinder's house, I met Ken Webster and Debbie Oaks. They shared a stack of papers they claimed had Elizabethan messages on them. I explained that if I take this case on, it would need to be on my own terms. They agreed. First, I needed to take all the printouts of these messages.

Back home, I was amazed at the sheer volume of the beautifully cursive calligraphy. I am not an Elizabethan scholar. I was unable to find one. In any case, I was not about to hire such a person. I do own a couple of Elizabethan books and some facsimile documents that I, as an amateur, was able to compare the style and wordage to. It all looked quite impressive to me.

I decided to conduct my own investigation of the cottage. As this phenomenon was centered around communications originally on a computer, I decided that I would use my own computer to investigate.

The whole of my tests and investigation were conducted using an early Tandy TRS-80 Level Two computer and printer connected to a home-built input output unit that autonomously controlled all sensors and printed out a timed moment-by-moment report and status. It was also connected to many other units, such as a video camera, recorder, audio tape recorder, and other specialized home-built units normally used when investigating. The equipment was all state-of-the-art for 1986.

This case turned out to be the world's first computer-controlled psychic investigation. All magnetic tapes were opened in the presence of Ken and Debbie and they signed them to confirm they were sealed and unopened prior to use.

Much later, I could freely communicate with 2109. Obviously, when confronted with the suggestion they were from the future, I was challenged to find ways to prove this outlandish claim. I am not at liberty to tell you exactly how I did this. I just ask you to take my word for it. The methods and questioning I used were solid. I can say "they" made communications possible in those not-so-technical days. In addition, they were able to put those messages into an undoctored BBC computer, despite it being inside of a Faraday shield and only connected to the electricity by a mains cleaner filter!

As unfathomable as it is for many people to believe, "they" knew all of my personal details. I mean personal. These were details that no one else but myself was privileged to know.

This case turned out to be one of the most challenging I ever investigated.

If you conclude it to be true, it provides the most serious implications for science and humanity.

If you conclude this a hoax, then you are forced to confess that it is the very best and most intricate and unnecessary falsifications ever. Good luck trying to make that explanation sound any more logical than the least likely explanation.

As for myself, I don't feel any compunction to prove it real or otherwise. Instead, I take comfort in knowing the knowledge will eventually be known to the world without me having to strike a blow.

Is Tomas Harden a Real Person from Dodleston?

Yes. The 1884 Oxford Historical Society records says this about Thomas (spelling modernized) Harden:

Four and a half years later, on December 17, 1538, a graduate in law of Brasenose, named George Munson or Mounson, laid an information before Richard Smyth, commissary of the Chancellor, that Thomas Harden, a Fellow of Brasenose and presumably Dean of the Chapel, had not, according to his duty ("ex officio"), deleted the name of the Pope "e quodam manual! Collegii." The significance of the deletion to Smyth is that the commissary was probably at that time already known for his leanings towards the new opinions which he subsequently embraced. "Harden," says Wood, "appeared so foul by some rash expressions dropt from his mouth, that he was cited soon after to appear before the King's Council to answer for what he had said and done."

Oxford Historical Society records of 1884.
Photo by Bill Hall.

Public Comments from a Friend of Frank Davies

This person claims to be a close friend of Frank Davies, a teacher and one of the first-hand witnesses of the Dodleston messages. He's an elderly man now, and the friend says he's one of the most honest men you will ever know. The anonymous friend hopes that someday Tomas's book will be found so the truth of this phenomena can be proven as genuine. No one knows when that will be, but the friend is confident it will eventually happen.

Swiss Bulletin for Parapsychology

The November 1986 edition of the *Swiss Bulletin for Parapsychology* said:

Of course, the fraud hypothesis was also considered, but rejected because of the numerous historical similarities and also the integrity of Webster and his colleagues. In England, all these phenomena were not given the necessary meaning, and Webster was very unhappy about them. Representatives of the SPR failed to analyze the computer printouts for their linguistic and historical accuracy. A specific review was rejected. Once again it became clear that people simply reject anything that does not fit into their world view.

Assuming that the material characteristics are historically verifiable, and fraud can be excluded, this is real phenomena, even if many people are burdened with the prejudice that cannot be what is not allowed to be. In particular, one cannot ignore phenomena that occur not only once at a certain place and not with just one particular person (see also Manfred Boden and Harsch-Fischbach).

Society of Psychical Research (SPR)

The SPR sent David Welch and physicist and computer expert Mr. John Bucknall to investigate. His goal was to perform eight detailed comprehensive examinations of the phenomena of Meadow Cottage. The primary experiment was the asking of ten special questions by typing them onto the computer screen to illicit a response.

"We did not get a specific answer," said Bucknall. "We got a generalized commentary accusing us of not believing in what was going on. We got waffle."

The reports at the time indicate John was not convinced anything paranormal was occurring, however, nothing was specifically debunked either.

"Something or someone is doing it," he said. Having once established to its satisfaction that human agencies were responsible, it was not the job of the Society (SPR) to point the finger."

He was also quoted in the media saying, "Clearly, if the case is a hoax, then the two teachers are prime suspects. I believe it is also possible that a third party was responsible. I would have loved to prove it was genuine. It would have been the most unique phenomenon ever recorded."

However, the SPR folks could not debunk or explain how any of it was done. Their theories consisted of blaming the neighbor without any evidence or indication, recording the tapping of the keyboard and then being able to convert the sound to the corresponding letters, and other far-reaching explanations. They did devote time to the case, but without staying over concurrent days, it made it difficult to catch the results to their satisfaction.

SPR witnessed the discovery of a message when Ken and Deb were not able to be suspects. The message made clear that the questions left in secret by the SPR on their own computer was read or known by the responder. Deb's mother was also a witness to messages, along with Peter Trinder, Frank Davis, and others. Still, the investigators were convinced it was a hoax. It appeared too unbelievable to accept for them.

Conclusions

When other Old English experts were consulted for a BBC special, they only looked at one message, and they were told it was for a paranormal documentary. The specimen used was the one that Tomas previously identified as not his, and he relayed that to Ken. They both thought that 2109 might have altered the message. The experiment ended up being biased. It didn't include the volumous collection of Old English messages that would have been more useful to examine. Either way, the analysis was further biased by disclosing that the messages were supposed to be paranormal.

Witness credibility and investigations, coupled with classic poltergeist activity, renders this case compelling and potentially genuine. It's not an easy one to believe based on the volume and various characters involved in the messages. If genuine, how would we know exactly who the authors of the messages were? Tomas appeared to be genuine. Ken and Deb think it just might be a person from the 16th century; most likely (as they later discovered) it would have been from around the year 1540.

CHARACTERISTICS

MESSAGE TYPE: COMPUTER, CHALK, LETTERS, DREAMS, AND INTERMEDIARY

FREQUENCY: MULTIPLE (VERY ACTIVE FOR SIXTEEN MONTHS)

OTHER PHENOMENA: YES (PART OF A POLTERGEIST INFESTATION)

FROM: TOMAS, 2109, UNKNOWN ENTITIES, AN EARLY COMPUTER WIZ IN AN UNMARKED VAN OUTSIDE THE COTTAGE? THE MOST INTRICATE, UNNECESSARY, AND UNREWARDING HOAX?

WITNESSES: YES (GARY ROWE, FRIENDS AND COLLEAGUES, SPR INVESTIGATORS)

ELEMENTS: THE EVENT WAS INVESTIGATED AND HAD MULTIPLE WITNESSES. IT OCCURRED WITHIN A POLTERGEIST INFESTATION, AND THE MESSAGE ACTIVITY CALMED THE OTHER PHYSICAL POLTERGEIST MANIFESTATIONS. KEN AND DEB WERE CONVINCED THAT TOMAS WAS NOT AN ENTITY IMPOSTER, BUT RATHER PART OF THE PHENOMENA FROM DIMENSIONS COLLIDING. KEN AND DEB HAVE NOT HAD ANY PARANORMAL EXPERIENCES BEFORE OR AFTER DODLESTON. THE COTTAGE ACTIVITY APPEARED TO CONTINUE IN SOME FORM FOR LATER RESIDENTS.

6

The Haunted Cable Box

The family you are about to read about will probably never say there's nothing interesting to watch on TV.
—Jimmy Petonito

Investigated by Jimmy Petonito and Rick Clark

On Tuesday, October 8, 1996, at 11 p.m., David, Ann, and their fifteen-year-old son David Jr. were watching *Seinfeld* together in the living room. Around 11:15 p.m., the cable box that sits next to their TV started changing stations, seemingly on its own. The chosen stations seemed random. David and Ann joked that maybe it was a spirit.

David figured he would test it out. He said, "If you're a spirit, go to channel 24." The cable box immediately switched to channel 24. The volume on the TV was fluctuating higher and lower for no logical reason. Their sole remote control for the cable box sat on the windowsill.

As a result of being frightened, they pulled the plug on the TV and wrapped a pair of jeans around the cable box so they didn't have to see the numbers change.

The next morning, they joked about it, saying it was probably just their imaginations or something wrong with the cable system or box. The next morning it was fine, but around the same time, 11:15 a.m., the box started changing stations again.

David Jr. suggested the cable box might be trying to communicate with them. It crossed his mind that perhaps it could be his cousin from Florida who committed suicide earlier that year.

The cable box rapidly raced from channels 72–0, faster than it would go if you held your finger on the remote.

David Jr. then suggested to tell it that channel 1 is "A," channel two is "B," channel 3 is "C," and so on. The cable box immediately switched to stations 25, 5, and then 19. Using the established code, this spelled out the word "yes." David, the father, began asking the TV set questions, wrote down the channels it went to and then decoded it afterward.

The cable box would address family members and visitors by their age. For example, when David walked in the room, the cable box would go to 44. This was interpreted as the spirit acknowledging him, saying hi. When a person would leave the room, it would flash their age three times. This was interpreted as "it" saying goodbye.

When the cable box wanted to initiate a conversation, it would flash "44," and David understood that to mean it wanted his attention to "talk." Neighbors visited to see the cable box in action. It knew the age of everyone that came to visit. It also revealed information like people's phone numbers, Social Security numbers, and other information that David and the family didn't have previous knowledge of or access to.

The cable box's answers revealed that a spirit was indeed trying to contact them. His name was Joseph Dana. Joseph claimed he was murdered in the apartment. David asked if it was a good spirit. It spelled out "yes."

Joseph Dana claimed he was shot in the same apartment they were in. He was shot in the head with a .45 caliber gun. He was killed on October 9, 1985. He said he was carried out of the apartment by three men in a rolled-up carpet and buried down the street under a porch. He even provided the house address.

David asked the spirit if he could get a copy of the death certificate. It answered no since it was never officially reported. Joseph explained he thought he was in purgatory. He could see both Jesus and Satan.

David asked how he could help him. Joseph responded he wanted a proper Christian burial. David felt this was a soul in need and wanted to help him. He then contacted the police. David wasn't afraid or frightened anymore; instead he wanted to help this poor soul.

The Haunted Cable Box

Officer Robert Nesci of the Meriden Police Department came to take a report. David told them the intricate story about the phenomena. He thought the information may hold a clue to solve a potential missing persons case.

David was showing the officer how the cable box would answer him at will. David asked Nesci to write his age on a piece of paper. The officer held a piece of paper close to his chest away from everyone and wrote it down; the cable box immediately went to that number. David then asked the box to describe the details about the alleged murder, and it performed in front of the police officers and told the same story. To prove this wasn't a hoax, David told everyone to put their hands in the air and he was giving mathematical problems for the cable box to solve (for example, what's two plus two, multiply that by six, divide that by three...), and the cable box immediately showed the correct answers. David asked how many people were in the room. The cable box responded "nine" (which was correct). He asked how many females were in the room. It responded "three," which was correct. This is all reflected in the police report. David also asked the spirit for his Social Security number, which it answered correctly.

Officer Nesci then called Lieutenant Frank Lewandowski to come to the house. It answered all the same questions for the lieutenant, but the lieutenant was skeptical. The fifteen-year-old son was sitting on the couch with a blanket on. The lieutenant told him to put the blanket down because he believed the son might be doing it. David Jr. took the blanket off, and that eliminated him from being the operator.

In a newspaper interview, the lieutenant said he believed someone was playing a practical joke and had another remote. David thought the officer was skeptical and would never be a believer, no matter what he witnessed.

Police officers went upstairs to make sure the woman on the second floor wasn't a party to a joke. They found no evidence to support it.

The police called the cable company. The next day, a technician came to the house and installed a new cable box. As soon as the technician left, it started flashing 44 again. However, the spirit did have a bit of trouble with the new box; it wasn't answering as quickly and smoothly as it did previously.

David asked Father Ed from St. Stanislas to come over to bless the house. The priest was at the home for twenty minutes and then the box started to perform. Dave claims the priest watched him communicate with the box for fifteen to twenty minutes and then said he had to get to a seminar and would return in a week. He promised to check in with the family then.

The family also contacted a detective. The missing persons case went cold when the family was told there was no one by that name ever reported missing. Also, the Social Security number given never existed.

We (Rick and Jimmy) were sent to the home to investigate. By the time we were contacted, it didn't use the TV to communicate anymore. An examination of their bookshelves revealed they had no visible magic or paranormal books. All family members reported hearing low guttural voices in a language they couldn't comprehend. Black shapes also moved from room to room. Items in the house were also springing to life and moving, such as the toaster.

We stayed at the house for three nights, determined to get the cable box to give messages by changing stations when we ask questions. We kept trying. We heard a response of sorts. The box made a noise from within—a clicking sound, but it was unable to change the stations. Rick and I heard a ruckus in the tiny closet behind the television. When we opened the closet door, there was nothing to be found, just clothes and the usual closet items. In Dave Jr.'s room, swirling black masses formed while the lights were off. The clouds were darker than the dark in the room and were moving around. Jimmy tried to capture them on video, but the camera wasn't good enough and it wouldn't focus well.

The family was terrified and afraid that no one could help them. Rick and Jimmy agreed to return the next evening and give the house a cleansing, a blessing, or whatever you want to call it.

When we arrived the next evening, David shared with us that the TV communicated again. Right before we arrived, the cable box kept blinking 66, 66, 66 and then gave one last message, "Look out tonight," which they interpreted as a warning.

David had the Bible on audio tape. The set was in a large clam shell case with many tapes in it. David asked if he could play this while we were doing the prayers. Rick said he could. Jimmy told them that doing this may be successful or the activity may pick up. David asked what tape I (Rick) wanted him to play. I pointed to the first one and said he could

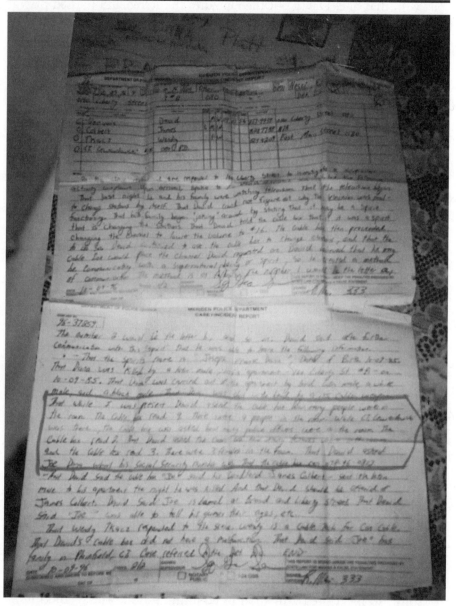

The police report filed regarding the cable box. *Photo by Jimmy Petonito.*

start with that one. David put the tape into the stereo and pressed play. It began playing backward. Hearing anything backward is creepy, but I even captured it on video. David tried the rest of the tapes and found them all to work properly except for the first one. After we finished, we left for the night. I called them the following morning to see if there was any activity. They didn't answer the phone that day. Or any other day. Their neighbors explained that they left abruptly from the house. It was described as quite rushed, looking like a couple on the run from the police.

We asked the family why they thought this activity suddenly started after living there for years with no activity. Dave Jr. finally confessed his fear of why this was all happening. When visiting his cousin in Florida last summer, he watched his cousin and his cousin's friends participate in a Satanic ritual, which involved the sacrifice of a goat.

The cable box messages lasted for only a few weeks. At the start, David believed it was a lost soul in need. By the end, he believed it was an entity just baiting him.

Police Report, October 9, 1996

At the above date and time, responded to [address] to investigate a suspicious activity complaint. Upon arrival, spoke to [name] and she relayed the following: That last night, he and his family were watching television. The television began to change channels by itself. David could not figure out why the television was malfunctioning. His family began "joking" around by stating that it may be a spirit that is changing the stations. David told the cable box, "If you're a spirit, go to channel 24." The cable box immediately switched to channel 24.

David continued to ask the cable box to change stations, and the cable box would switch to the channels David requested. David believed that he may be communicating with a supernatural or spirit, so he created a method of communication. The method is as follows: The number 1 will be the letter A, the number 2 would be the letter B, and so on. David said after further communication with this "spirit," he was able to learn the following information. The spirits name is Joseph Frank Dana, date of birth 10/9/45.

Dana was killed by a Latin male in his apartment [address], on 10/9/85. Dana was carried out of the apartment by said Latin male, a white male, and a black male. Dana was shot in the head by a .45 caliber weapon.

While I was present, David asked the cable box how many people were in the room. The cable box read 9. There were 9 people in the room. While Lieutenant [name] was there, the cable box was asked how many police officers were in the room. The cable box read 2. David asked the cable box how many females were in the room, and the cable box read 3. There were 3 females in the room. David asked Joe Dana what his social security card is and the cable box communicated ###-##-####. David said the cable box "Joe" said the landlord James Colbert sent the Latin male to his apartment the night he was killed, and David should be afraid of James Colbert. David said Joe is buried at Broad and Liberty Street. David said "Joe" was able to tell his guests their ages, etc.

Wendy [name] responded to the scene. Wendy is a cable tech for Cox Cable. David's cable box did not have a malfunction. David said "Joe" has family in Plainfield, Connecticut. Case referred to the Detective. END.

The haunted cable box. *Photo by Jimmy Petonito.*

CHARACTERISTICS

MESSAGE TYPE: CABLE BOXES (TWO DIFFERENT ONES)

FREQUENCY: MULTIPLE

OTHER PHENOMENA: NO BUT UNSURE WITH THE FAMILY LEAVING SUDDENLY; IT'S POSSIBLE THE ACTIVITY COULD HAVE ESCALATED.

FROM: UNKNOWN ENTITY

WITNESSES: YES (FAMILY, INVESTIGATORS, POLICE OFFICERS)

ELEMENTS: QUESTION AND ANSWER; FAMILY WOULD HAVE BEEN SUSPECT, BUT OTHER PHENOMENA TOOK PLACE AND THEY MOVED ABRUPTLY DUE TO THE ACTIVITY.

ELECTRONIC ASSESSMENT: THE BIBLE AUDIO BOOK COULD HAVE BEEN A STROKE OF POOR TIMING BY PLAYING A CASSETTE THAT MIGHT HAVE HAD A TWIST IN THE TAPE, CAUSING IT TO PLAY BACKWARD. OR MAYBE IT DOESN'T. WE DON'T WANT TO BREAK THE TAPE, BEING A KEEPSAKE FROM THE CASE. SINCE IT'S ONLY A SMALL PART OF THE ENTIRE EVENT, IT'S NOT A CRITICAL PIECE. THAT'S WHY WE ALWAYS SUGGEST THAT EVERY SINGLE INDICATOR OF THE PARANORMAL BE TESTED ON ITS OWN MERITS.

7

EXTRATERRESTRIALS

The basic rules for these arrogant opinion setters are: 1. Don't bother me with the facts, my mind is made up; 2. What the public doesn't know, I won't tell them; 3. If one can't attack the data, attack the people, it is easier; and 4. Do "research" by proclamation rather than admitting ignorance and doing a serious investigation.
—Stanton Friedman

Alleged alien messages often take the form of communication via a dream state, medium, or telepathically. We will include cases that have some of these components, however, we want to focus on other messaging without an intermediary. Like other cases, experiences that are part of additional phenomena offer support and intrigue that are worthy of careful consideration.

Phantom phone calls are commonplace in conjunction with UFO encounters. Haunted houses, cryptid sightings, and even poltergeist activity can be the result of, or accompany, UFO incidents. These calls might take the form of a warning not to discuss their experience, or from what appears to be extraterrestrial voices themselves. Sometimes they follow the tell-tale signs of the real Men in Black, Women in Black, or children of the grey descriptions. Radio stations will report programming interrupted by "electronic tones" during UFO sighting activity.

Phone interference is also a familiar characteristic of many UFO experiencers. The calls are often untraceable. They can originate from the extraterrestrials themselves or the sightings can be accompanied by calls from strange humanoids—robotic sounding "people" warning the witnesses not to discuss what they have experienced. In addition to warning calls, experiencers might receive a call from an odd person that starts interviewing them. The voices are described as something pretending to be human but not quite correct; something is *off*. The interview questions are also weird and incorporate different names for people or places not used in common conversation, along with other abnormal word choice and usage. This fits the common extraterrestrial weakness: difficulty in imitating us accurately enough so we don't sense it. The Men in Black (MIB) witnesses repeatedly report them driving old cars that look (and smell, if you end up inside) brand new. Their clothes are not typical for modern wear. It's simply not quite up to date, but also looks brand new. They miss the mark on behavior too, because they communicate in person in the same unnatural way as over the phone. The MIB might say they are from the government or a newspaper, but the contact name given doesn't exist when the witnesses check into it.

Alien illustration. *Courtesy of Heidi Petonito.*

Despite widespread belief in the idea of finding life on other planets, we have failed to provide evidence that would conclusively determine that intelligent contact is unquestionable. If you ask experiencers, individuals who have personally experienced encounters and/or abductions, there is no question it happened. Who they are, what they want, where they come from, and other basic questions are likely to remain until we can produce something revealing for scientists to examine. Perhaps an advanced implant? Or other foreign object made of a substance not found here?

Until the time comes for certainty, we have some interesting testimony that we will share as we explore phantom messages related to the UFO phenomena.

Phone Calls from a Spacecraft
Jack Sarfatti
Brooklyn, New York, 1952
Story courtesy of Jack Sarfatti from his book *Destiny Matrix*

I was reading a book on computer switching circuits at home when the phone rang. I answered it and heard a strange sequence of clunking mechanical sounds. Then a metallic sounding voice comes on the line. A cold mechanical voice is the only way I can describe it. It gives a long series of numbers that I did not understand and then calls me Jack and says it's a "conscious computer on board a spacecraft." It may have said it was from the future, but I am not sure. However, that was the implication of what it said. Anyway, it says I've been selected to be one of "400 young receptive minds" to be part of a special project, but that I must make the choice myself. The voice on the phone told me that I would begin to meet the others I was to work with in twenty years. I was scared and everything in me screamed to say NO! and hang up. I felt a strong jolt of electricity go up my spine to the base of my skull, and I heard myself say YES. I was terrified and fascinated.

The voice said, "Good. Go out on your fire escape and we will send a ship to pick you up in ten minutes."

When I hung up, I ran like a bat out of hell and found my friend Winky, who is now a homicide detective in Brooklyn. We, and a few other kids, went back to my apartment to wait for the flying saucer. It never came.

I was stunned. I only remembered one phone call. I still only remember one call. My mother told me there were frequent calls over a three-week period. She said I was walking around glassy-eyed. Finally, she picked up the phone and listened out of concern for me. She heard the cold mechanical voice. She told it to quit bothering me and stop calling. The calls stopped.

Those phone calls were instrumental in Jack becoming a physicist, and a rather revolutionary one who advanced quantum research. Jack has no idea if these calls really were from a spacecraft or whether they were a cruel practical joke. Either way, they changed Jack's life forever.

CHARACTERISTICS

MESSAGE TYPE: LANDLINE PHONE

FREQUENCY: MULTIPLE

OTHER PHENOMENA: NO

FROM: EXTRATERRESTRIAL

WITNESSES: YES (MOM)

ELEMENTS: METALLIC VOICE. THIS IS A FAMILIAR DESCRIPTION IN THE UFO PHENOMENA. THE VOICES/SOUNDS ARE OFTEN DESCRIBED AS "METALLIC" OR "INSECT-LIKE" OR BOTH.

The Mothman Messages
John Keel
Point Pleasant, West Virginia, 1966

In Point Pleasant, West Virginia, during 1966 and 1967, about 200 witnesses experienced some form of strange phenomena. UFOs, animal mutilations, and the sighting of the mysterious creature coined "The Mothman" was encountered by more than a hundred individuals. It was often described as six or seven feet tall with red eyes and no head, as if the eyes were in the breast area. The creature had huge wings.

One version of the frequently sighted Mothman. *Illustration by Mike Mendes.*

John Keel visited Point Pleasant to investigate and interview eyewitnesses of the entity. In 1975, he published the famous book about the phenomenon entitled *The Mothman Prophecies*.

As part of the events that happened there, both John and others received bizarre phone calls that mirror other UFO-related contacts. Many readers will know the story, but if you do not, we highly recommend that you read Mr. Keel's now infamous treatise on this incredible case.

A Mothman Phantom Message Example

Jane answered a call, and a strange metallic voice addressed her.

"Listen carefully," it said. "I cannot hear you."

It instructed her to go to a library nearby and reference a chosen book on Indian history. She followed this weird request. The library was empty, except for the librarian. Jane saw the lady and thought she was unusual. The woman was "dressed in an old-fashioned suit like something out of the

1940s, with a long skirt, broad shoulders, and flat, old-looking shoes. She had a dark complexion, with a fine bone structure, and very black eyes and hair." The woman also seemed to be expecting her arrival. She produced the book in question instantly from under her desk. Jane sat down at a table and began to riffle through the book, pausing on page 42. Her caller had told her to read that page.

"You won't believe this, but the print became smaller and smaller, then larger and larger. It changed into a message and I can remember every word of it:

> Good morning, friend. You have been selected for many reasons. One is that you are advanced in autosuggestion. Through this science, we will make contact. I have messages concerning Earth and its people. The time is set. Fear not . . . I am a friend. For reasons best known to ourselves, you must make your contacts known to one reliable person. To break this code is to break contact. Proof shall be given. Notes must be kept of the suggestion state. Be in peace, [signed] A Pal."

A John Keel Time Slip Phantom Message Example

"We've got a lot of messages here for you, Mr. Keel," she said, pulling out a sheet of message slips.

"I started to protest since I had not even known I was going to stay at that motel until minutes before. The messages were all nonsensical, meant only to prove once more that my movements were being anticipated," Keel writes.

John continued to investigate the unknown, and he was well versed in the study of weird phone calls relating to the UFO phenomenon. Calls have been described as having mechanical sounds, high-pitched sounds, and the familiar beeping tones.

CHARACTERISTICS

MESSAGE TYPE: LANDLINE PHONES

FREQUENCY: MULTIPLE

OTHER PHENOMENA: YES (MOTHMAN FLAP AREA)

FROM: EXTRATERRESTRIAL, UNKNOWN ENTITY

WITNESSES: NO (MANY WITNESSES TO THE MOTHMAN PHENOMENA, HOWEVER)

ELEMENTS: METALLIC VOICE. THIS IS A FAMILIAR DESCRIPTION IN UFO PHENOMENA. VOICES/SOUNDS ARE OFTEN DESCRIBED AS "METALLIC," "INSECT-LIKE," OR BOTH. A FLAP AREA IS INVOLVED, WHICH MAKES THE BIZARRE EVENTS FIT.

Otherworldly Phone Calls
Dr. Karla Turner
Denton, Texas, 1987

Dr. Karla Turner earned a PhD in Old English studies and was a college professor in Texas for more than a decade. She is also the author of *Taken* and *Into the Fringe*.

Dr. Turner received two mysterious phone calls at different times following her discovery that she and her husband Elton may have been abducted by aliens. Her death is surrounded with mystery and questions left unanswered.

Karla was in perfect health, and she had no history of cancer in her family. But on January 10, 1996, Karla died at the young age of forty-eight from an unidentified fast-acting cancer.

Our story begins with Elton driving home from the grocery store. He witnessed a giant spherical metallic object hovering over the town courthouse. It hovered stationary, with no sound whatsoever. Returning home with the groceries, he then walked up a nearby hill to get a better look at the object that remained in place over the courthouse.

Elton stood enamored by the copper-like object for about ten minutes.

Dr. Karla Turner. *Photo courtesy of Elton Turner.*

When he left the house to go look at the object, it was still light out. When he walked back home a short distance, he realized the sun was now going down and it was quickly getting dark. He was only on the hill for ten minutes, but Elton realized he was missing forty-five minutes. He had no way to account for this missing time.

Upon Karla's arrival home, Elton immediately shared his experience. Karla surmised it might be a movie prop. Many production companies film in that area, so it was a logical conclusion. Looking for more clues, they scoured the newspapers the following week to see if there were any other sightings or information regarding a movie filming.

After two days passed, Elton discovered a long scab on the back of his leg. He had no idea when, how, or where he could have obtained such a scab.

Soon after the scab incident, both Karla and Elton began having physical and mental troubles. Karla developed TMJ, a condition she never had at any point in her life. Elton experienced sudden numbness and tingling in the same leg and area that the scab appeared. In addition, he also started suffering from severe headaches, coupled with stomach pains. The couple both exhibited symptoms of acute stress without being able to understand or determine the source of such trauma.

Karla made an appointment with her physician to seek relief for her newfound stress. She also visited a psychiatrist regarding her problem. Neither one could pinpoint the cause or source of why she would suddenly experience these symptoms.

Karla sought a counselor who taught her a simple autosuggestion technique to help her relax by redirecting her thoughts and energy toward a more positive direction.

Meanwhile, Elton was suffering through his acute stress. Karla thought the technique might help Elton, even though she only started to use it herself.

Elton agreed to try to use this relaxation technique. He laid down on the couch, relaxing his body. Karla witnessed him entering a trance-like state. Suddenly, appearing startled, he raised off the couch in one single motion from his horizontal starting position.

He let out a cry for help, and then said, "I see a face. I see a gigantic ship in the sky. It's the size of a small city!"

Right then, their phone rang. Karla reached for the phone and answered it with the usual hello. Hearing no one on the other end, she repeated her greeting: "Hello? Hello?" There still was no reply. Then a voice started to emit from the line, one she could only describe as an angry voice. It sounded like metallic, insectoid chattering. Following her hearing this sound, Elton snapped out of his trance. The line went dead.

Puzzled by this ever-evolving series of bizarre events, they began to consider regression techniques. They discovered that they may have been both plagued by these encounters since early childhood.

Dr. Turner initiated working with experiencers, specifically people who claimed to be abductees. In January of 1994, she was talking on the phone with Angie from Tennessee, one of the subjects she was interviewing for her book *Taken*.

Dr. Turner described the experience: "We were on the phone. Both of our phones were regular phones, and in the course of our conversation, Angie was telling me about a recent abduction experience in which a particular group of humanoids (allegedly hybrids) were with her at a facility and they told her they came from the area of Cassiopeia, the constellation."

She said to Karla, "Do you think this could be true?"

Karla said, "There's no way of knowing. They've told us they're from Mars and all different kinds of alleged places. There's no way of knowing and there's no reason to believe or disbelieve without some sort of confirmation."

At that point in the conversation, there was an electronic zip sound on our phone and a clear male voice came on the line that may or may not be human.

It said, "There's a lot of them out there and we know where they come from!"

Both heard the voice, followed by yet another electric zip sound. The "man" was gone. Dr. Brown picked up the phone off the floor, which marked the end of the strange encounter.

Prior to their first incident, they never had any issues. Following their first incident, they now found unmarked cars circling their neighborhood, along with helicopters flying over their house—at times as many as nine of them. This occurred frequently and almost continuously. Their mail was also intercepted and tampered with.

Dr. Turner was ultimately threatened and then contracted cancer. Other experiencers that she was working with also were threatened before contracting cancer and meeting untimely quick deaths.

CHARACTERISTICS

Message Type: Landline phone

Frequency: Twice

Other Phenomena: Yes (UFO)

From: Extraterrestrial, unknown entity

Witnesses: Yes (Angie)

Elements: The familiar reporting of insect-like sounds.

Signal Anomalies May Be from Extraterrestrial Intelligence
Ermanno F. Borra and Eric Trottier
2016

In October of 2016, while many people were gearing up for an election, Ermanno F. Borra and Eric Trottier published their findings. Although not conclusive, this is the most promising evidence of potential contact that we've ever had. Here's what happened, along with the actual abstract reproduced on page 126 and 127 for any science buffs out there (or actual scientists).

The paper is entitled "Discovery of Peculiar Periodic Spectral Modulations in a Small Fraction of Solar Type Stars." Don't worry, we'll explain. In 2012, Ermanno suggested that extraterrestrial intelligence (ETI) could send pairs of light pulses separated by a constant time interval to generate periodic spectral modulations. In other words, they could send us signals at equal repetitive intervals, and we would hopefully know it's not normal space stuff. The aliens would use these signals to make us aware of their existence and send us messages. That's if we could figure out a code we both can understand.

Borra uses computer simulations to create the stars and the modulation to mimic how we could expect an alien intelligence to signal us. Just a few years later, the hypothesized signals were received for real.

The signal is not visible in the noisy frequency spectrum. The detected signals have identical characteristics of the signals predicted. The signals are also of a narrow width. This makes sense versus sending a stronger signal. If the aliens have advanced technology, they consequently might have extremely powerful sources. There may be several reasons. First, sending a stronger signal requires more energy, which has obvious inconveniences, particularly if you consider signals sent to a very large number of stars.

These creatures probably know about wavelengths too and therefore would know we can detect weak signals, like they did. They might know that technologically advanced civilizations can have powerful telescopes that can discover weak signals.

Only a small number of stars in a narrow range are centered near a star that is similar to our sun. This provides us with messages that mirror the extraterrestrial intelligence hypothesis. In other words, we would expect that similar stars (or suns) would potentially have life nearby, but only a small fraction of them. And we currently have the technology to send signals having the energy needed to be detected 1,000 light years away. Obviously, more advanced civilizations would have technologies capable of generating much stronger signals.

Borra illustrates this by asking us to imagine how this would have been received if he submitted his research in 1950, before the invention of the laser, when it would have suggested the use of a light bulb to send the signal.

He cautions that this hypothesis needs to be confirmed with further work. This can be done by repeatedly observing the stars in question with photoelectric detectors capable of detecting very rapid intensity signals. Aliens may not necessarily send us signals 24/7/365, so even with no signal, there might still be life. Borra also postulates that other life-forms might add more information in the signals by sending pairs of pulses separated by the same time intervals, but with the pairs sent in a Morse-like code to send us messages or perhaps even pictures of themselves.

Borra sums it up nicely: "At this point, the ETI hypothesis is the only one that stands. However, it is such a peculiar hypothesis that it must be confirmed with more work."

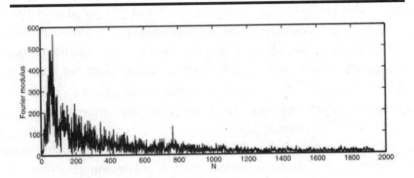

Illustration of statistically significant anomalous activity from an F5 star that may be of intelligent origin. *Illustration courtesy of Ermanno F. Borra.*

We asked Ermanno about his personal belief about the possibility of extraterrestrial life:

As an astronomer, I think that it is almost certain. However, from what I have read, if you ask the question to an astronomer, he would answer that it is certain because he knows that there is an extremely large number of stars similar to the sun. If you ask the question to a biologist, he would answer that it is highly unlikely because the probability of life generation is virtually 0.0. Finally, I think that the fact there is life on Earth definitely shows that life exists in planets in solar-like stars.

The following is the official abstract for the research.

Discovery of Peculiar Periodic Spectral Modulations in a Small Fraction of Solar Type Stars

E. F. Borra, E. Trottier

Département de Physique, Université Laval, Québec, QC G1V 0A6, Canada;
Received 2015 December 9; accepted 2016 June 20; published 2016 October 14

A Fourier transform analysis of 2.5 million stars in the Sloan Digital Sky Survey was carried out to detect periodic spectral modulations. Signals having the same period were found in only 234 stars overwhelmingly in the F2 to K1 spectral range. The signals cannot be caused by instrumental or data analysis effects because they are present in only a very small fraction of stars within a narrow spectral range and because signal to noise ratio considerations predict that the signal should mostly be detected in the brightest objects, while this is not the case. We consider several possibilities, such as rotational transitions in molecules, rapid pulsations, Fourier transform of spectral lines and signals generated by Extraterrestrial Intelligence (ETI). They cannot be generated by molecules or rapid pulsations. It is highly unlikely that they come from the Fourier transform of spectral lines because too many strong lines located at nearly periodic frequencies are needed. Finally, we consider the possibility, predicted in a previous published paper, that the signals are caused by light pulses generated by Extraterrestrial Intelligence to makes us aware of their existence. We find that the detected signals have exactly the shape of an ETI signal predicted in the previous publication and are therefore in agreement with this hypothesis. The fact that they are only found in a very small fraction of stars within a narrow spectral range centered near the spectral type of the sun is also in agreement with the ETI hypothesis. However, at this stage, this hypothesis needs to be confirmed with further work. Although unlikely, there is also a possibility that the signals are due to highly peculiar chemical compositions in a small fraction of galactic halo stars.

Note: This research has been supported by the Natural Sciences and Engineering Research Council of Canada. Funding for SDSS-III has been provided by the Alfred P. Sloan Foundation, the Participating Institutions, the National Science Foundation, and the US Department of Energy Office of Science. The SDSS-III website is *www.sdss3.org*.

An Alien Entity Caught on X-Ray

Jimmy's friend Jack (pseudonym) works at a hospital and a doctor passed on an X-ray to him. The radiologist knew Jack investigated the paranormal, and this X-ray was quite unusual. It had a humanoid inside of it; or at least it appeared to have a figure in there.

We had others look at it, including a radiologist. It's an X-ray of the odontoid: a cervical spine view and a skull view. The independent radiologist not part of the X-ray exchange believes it is an "artifact." In other words, it's two images, one placed over the other. The X-ray is legit, but not the skeleton image.

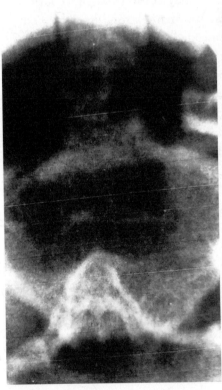

X-ray with humanoid figure. *Courtesy of Jack.*

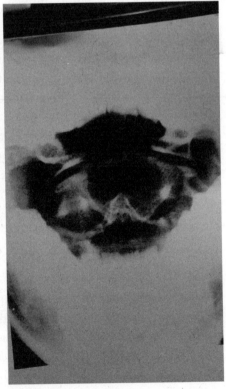

Normal X-ray with the correct area remaining black. *Courtesy of Jack.*

Bill's friend Dianne, who is a radiologic technologist/CAT scan technologist, had another idea of what might be the cause for this unusual image. Her thought eliminates a prank or trick, and instead is the result of misinterpretation. Dianne says it looks like an image was taken and then another image was taken, resulting in a double exposure. That can happen by accident when using cassettes with film. Today, cassettes on film are no longer used because it's all digital. In this case, the two exposures showed up on the one film when processed.

It appears that there is no alien this time. We include this example because we find that a lot of so-called evidence is never vetted with the proper professionals. If you're no optic expert, stay away from announcing your unexplainable photo. Try to disprove or find a simple explanation for things that puzzle us. The other reason we include it? It's an incredible result and suitable for framing.

Alien Crisis Averted
Heather Wade
Merced, California, 2011

This is the first time Heather has shared her entire experience. She told us how it all started: "It was the summer of 2011, and as usual, I couldn't sleep. I'm a total insomniac. I'd been trying for hours to fall asleep. I finally said to hell with this. I'm going to take a walk."

At about 3:30 a.m., Heather started on her walk. The neighborhood was quiet. Desolate. Peaceful.

"Some movement in the sky catches my eye. I see this very bright light. It looks like a star but much brighter. I felt a flash of light hit my face," she explained.

Although she thinks exhaustion and mind tricks were to blame, her gaze could not turn away. Heather continued peering deep into the light. It seemed far away. A bright white light. What could it be? Heather figured it was probably a satellite, but that theory disintegrated fast.

Suddenly, the light began to move erratically. First it darted side to side, then figure-eight patterns, and finally moved in a circular pattern. It seemed to be saying 'Hey! Look at me up here!' Then it gets to the crazy part. I started getting thoughts in my head that weren't my own. There were flashes of images, technical information about propulsion, and how to travel between planets.

She couldn't place where these thoughts could have originated. This is not information that she stored or that she knew. Heather then felt a headache coming on. This was all too fantastic to take in. She looked around in hopes that another witness could help make sense of this night visitor. But she was alone. There was not another person in sight in any direction.

As all these thoughts raced in her head, her gaze remained fixed on this unidentified flying whatever. Whatever it was, it wasn't going away. Moving all around the sky like it owned it, this "thing" continued to seemingly taunt her. Finally, it darted away at an incredible speed, disappearing into the night sky.

Again, Heather ran through possibilities. That was no airplane, not a helicopter, not a drone, nothing imaginable. What in the world was that?

Both confused and drained of energy, Heather walked back home while trying to clear her mind of the incomprehensible encounter. A headache slowly grew again, as if determined to overtake her before she reached the house.

Back home, sleep did not come easy. The headache was at full strength and it still wasn't at its worst. She took Benadryl. Finally, some sleep was possible.

The next day, Heather carried on as usual, but with the night's adventure actively looming at the forefront of her mind. It was probably just a weird thing or a trick of the light. Who knows? She was positive there had to be a scientific explanation—a mundane explanation—for what was seen.

Heather continued,

I start to do work around my house. I notice a rough patch of skin in the middle of my left forearm. Hey, that's kind of weird. I'm scratching the rough patch on my skin and discover there is *something* underneath. I grab hold of a grain-sized object with the consistency of sand and rolled it between my finger and thumb. My thoughts jumped in again: This was definitely something that was not there before.

Was she abducted? She didn't think so. It was simply a weird light seen in the sky. At least that's the story she tried to sell herself.

This object was so small, it fell easily from her grasp to the light beige carpet. Well that's that, she thought. There was no hope of finding it now.

130

Almost instantly after dropping the unknown substance, the nasty headache made a marked improvement. She vacuumed up the area where it dropped and then took out the vacuum bag. The bag was then brought to the farthest dumpster she could find. Walking back home from her mission, the headache gradually subsided.

Heather Wade. *Courtesy of Heather Wade.*

"I have always been a quick healer, but this little spot took over three weeks to heal! Even after healing, it still left a dark red mark. Six years later and you could still see a little scar," she said.

The memorable part that reinforced the reality of this experience was the phantom messages. One in particular stands out: "We are trying to contact you. We're trying to contact different people to see if anyone can answer us."

Heather describes the moment: "I thought to myself, you've got the wrong person. I remember that was my last thought before the one-of-a-kind visitor(s) dashed away into nothingness."

When Jimmy had Heather as a guest on his radio show, he said this: "These beings travel galaxies and galaxies to communicate with you and you foiled them with a Hoover!"

CHARACTERISTICS

MESSAGE TYPE: SPACECRAFT

FREQUENCY: ONCE

OTHER PHENOMENA: YES (UFO, POTENTIAL IMPLANT)

FROM: EXTRATERRESTRIAL

WITNESSES: NO

ELEMENTS: THE COMBINATION OF A SIGHTING, MESSAGE, POTENTIAL IMPLANT, AND PHYSICAL EFFECTS.

Phone Calls Interrupted by Aliens
Betty Andreasson
South Ashburnham, Massachusetts, 1967

The classic alien abduction case known by the book of the same name, *The Andreasson Affair*, included strange phone calls by extraterrestrials.

Betty was on a phone call with Bob, a fellow witness and presumed experiencer, when a strange voice interrupted their call. It was a male voice described by Betty as "livid with anger," and it spoke in a truly foreign tongue. Clicking and tones were heard on the line. Experiencing vivid flashbacks, she advised Bob to hang up the call.

Raymond Fowler interviewed Betty in detail about the incident.

"It was a different language. There were a lot of L's and a lot of T's in it and a lot of rolling sounds. It was fast, like a record was put on fast speed, but even though it was fast, the words were very clear," Betty explained.

Bob could hear the voice, but could not understand the language spoken. Betty was getting nervous and upset and said she wanted to cry. It was something they said: "It is done. It is finished."

Betty heard the noises of heavy machinery on the phone, as if they were setting something up. Then the noises would stop, and they would speak again. She used the descriptor "insect-like," which is used a lot to when describing the sounds heard from alleged aliens. She also described the sounds as "a mad hornet or an ant gouging away at something." The voice kept spouting out words and repeating them over and over.

The strange tones heard on that phone call were familiar sounds. Betty heard them before. They interrupted her radio, and the tones played through her speakers.

This experience left Betty shaken and she had a deep feeling of dread. Twenty-four hours later, the newspaper headlines read "Westminster Crash Kills Two Brothers." Shortly before midnight on the same day of the terrifying phone call, her twenty-one-year-old son James and seventeen-year-old son Todd were killed in a car accident. Was the accident caused by extraterrestrials? Or were they warning Betty of impending danger to those closest to her?

The December 21, 1967, edition of the *Harold Journal* carried a story eerily similar. After a terrifying close encounter, Rita Mallery's car was taken over by a craft and eased into a nearby field. A light came down and her son appeared to suddenly be in a state of suspended animation.

She describes the incident:

Then I began to hear voices. They didn't sound like male or female voices, but were weird, the words broken and jerky…like a weird chorus of several voices. The voices named someone I knew and said that at that moment, my friend's brother was involved in a terrible accident miles away. They said my son would not remember any of this.

CHARACTERISTICS

MESSAGE TYPE: LANDLINE PHONE, RADIO

FREQUENCY: ONCE (BUT WITH A POTENTIAL RELATED INCIDENT)

OTHER PHENOMENA: YES (PART OF A VAST ABDUCTION EXPERIENCE)

FROM: EXTRATERRESTRIAL

WITNESSES: YES (BOB)

ELEMENTS: VOICE DESCRIBED AS HIGH-PITCHED, INSECT-LIKE, WITH TONES PLAYED. WARNING OR KILLERS?

Baby Learns "Alien Speak" from Phone Calls
Kathie Davis
Copley Woods, Indiana, 1983
An excerpt from *Intruders* by Budd Hopkins

Well-known abduction investigator Budd Hopkins investigated Kathie's case. (Her name was changed to protect her identity, but it was later revealed to be Debbie Jordan-Kauble, who is a member of MENSA. For cohesiveness with Hopkins's book, we'll use the name Kathie.) She experienced encounters all her life: sightings, abductions, and phantom messages.

She was pregnant with her second son when the one-of-a-kind phone calls began. On a Wednesday at 3 p.m., Kathie received the first of many otherworldly phone calls.

She picks up and hears what was described "like a factory in full swing" with a voice "moaning and muttering" but using no understandable syllables. Thinking it was a prank call, she asked who was calling several times. Getting no response, she hung up the phone and put it out of her mind.

The following Wednesday at 3 p.m., the mystery caller is back. Odd noises and moaning permeate the call. She listened for a bit and then hung up. The pattern had begun. Each Wednesday at 3 p.m., the same call was received. Her mother answered one of the calls and also heard "guttural" voices, along with roaring and clicking noises. A friend also answered one of the calls and heard the same strange things.

Kathie got an unlisted number that went into effect on a Monday. The next day, the phantom caller rang a day early. It was angry. That's the only call not to occur on a Wednesday. They continued for her entire pregnancy and then stopped.

She gave birth to a healthy baby boy. By three years old, however, his speech was not developing normally. He would moan! It sounded like an imitation of the extraterrestrial's voice. After consulting doctors, he was again affirmed to be healthy. Luckily, he grew out of the speech issue. Kathie knew that this was all related to her UFO experiences and the strange pregnancy caller.

CHARACTERISTICS

MESSAGE TYPE: LANDLINE PHONE

FREQUENCY: MULTIPLE (NINE MONTHS OF CALLS EVERY WEDNESDAY, EXCEPT FOR THE TUESDAY CALL)

OTHER PHENOMENA: YES (PART OF A VAST ABDUCTION EXPERIENCE)

FROM: EXTRATERRESTRIAL

WITNESSES: YES (MOM)

ELEMENTS: HER SON IMITATED THE PHONE VOICES AS A YOUNG CHILD.

The 1970s Alien Transmission
Colin Andrews

Colin Andrews is a well-known researcher and author and is widely acknowledged as the world expert on the crop circle phenomenon. It all began in 1983 when he was enroute to a meeting and saw a crop circle. Colin thought he should look into it. We are glad he did.

He is founder of Circles Phenomenon Research International, the first organization established specifically to investigate the crop circle phenomenon. His scientific investigations are responsible for much of the current information on the subject. Andrews supervised the largest surveillance project of its kind, Operation Blackbird, in 1990.

Andrews is an electrical engineer by profession and a former senior officer in British regional government.

I usually have a rather jaundiced view of UFO "contactee" claims, regardless of the country in which the claim is made, but there's something about the story told by professor Rodolfo Paredes (in the report provided by professor Ana Luisa Cid) that triggered a recollection. Whether or not Paredes is really in contact with "beings from Jupiter" is debatable, but the fact that they endeavor to make contact through his radio signal (it is unclear if Cid meant a "HAM radio" frequency or something else) is very interesting. In the late 1970s, Puerto Rican UFO researcher Orlando Rimax played a recording of an alleged alien transmission on his Otros Mundos broadcast, which aired every Sunday morning in the city of San Juan. The recording could have been a hoax, naturally, but the heavily distorted voice of a being calling itself "Omicron" was definitely disturbing.

It had a quality often associated with recorded sounds involving hauntings and paranormal goings-on, even though the entity professed an interplanetary origin, and they always do.

Back in 2003, I penned an article entitled "Spirit of the Radio" in which I discussed these broadcasts from allegedly nonhuman sources:

The purported space entity (meaning Omicron, from Rimax's 1977 radio program) had been picked up by a HAM radio operation, and it seemed to be taking a great deal of time establishing its nonhuman bona fides. Intrusions such as this one appear to be frequent in contactee circles; they are often dismissed as hoaxes, but they are nonetheless intriguing.

In the latest reissue of George Hunt Williamson's classic contactee work "Other Flesh, Other Voices," UFO author and publisher Timothy Green Beckley makes the interesting note that Williamson was a HAM operator "who claimed contact with extraterrestrial beings who were continually broadcasting messages from spaceships circling in the Earth's uppermost atmosphere."

In January 1971, a call-in show on Greater London Radio received a call from a "cold metallic voice" claiming to be of extraterrestrial origin. The voice, which did not give itself a name, said it was speaking by thought transference guided by computer and imparted the usual patter about the difficulties of life on Earth and humanity's unwillingness to forsake its primitive ways. When asked by the program's host if it was possible for humans to see the interstellar interlocutor, it replied that it was "possible to assume human appearance" for a specific number of minutes.

The ubiquitous Ashtar Command, a source of "space brother" wisdom for many decades, apparently transcended wireless to appear on the small screen. The Command hijacked a number of transmitters belonging to the Southern ITV network at 5:12 p.m. on November 26, 1977, broadcasting its message directly over a news broadcast. The network appears to have been unaware of the problem at the time, or completely unable to correct it. One possibility mentioned was that this was because the source of the overriding signal was not terrestrial in nature.

The message went on for a little over five minutes and contained a familiar warning: "We come to warn you of the destiny of your race and your world so that you may communicate to your fellow beings the course you must take to avoid the disasters which threaten your world, and the beings on our worlds around you. This is in order that you may share in the great awakening, as the planet passes into the New Age of Aquarius. The New

Age can be a time of great peace and evolution for your race, but only if your rulers are made aware of the evil forces that can overshadow their judgments."

Putting the New Age aside for a moment, it is nonetheless interesting that radio is somehow permeable to these entities. One of the most intriguing ongoing situations in South American ufology involves the activities of a group calling itself "Friendship," hailing from one of the many islands of the Chonos Archipelago and variously associated with UFO aliens, interdimensional beings, holdovers from Nazi Germany, and meddlesome CIA agents, depending on who is writing the article. In 1984, a HAM radio operator of by the name of Octavio Ortiz, a married resident of Santiago de Chile and proud owner of a 27 megacycle CB base station with which he talks to DXers all over the world, became the protagonist of a drama that unfolds to this very day.

That year, Ortiz received a distress call from a vessel that claimed to be ensnared by a mysterious light that was playing havoc with the ship's electronics. The light—an unknown craft—descended even lower over the vessel. Bewildered, Ortiz offered to retransmit messages to the authorities of the port of Iquique on behalf of the ship's master. As a result of this, Ortiz struck up a friendship with the ship's master, a man named Alberto, who told him that he had been recruited by mysterious "gringos" to ferry equipment and supplies to their mysterious island. These elusive northerners described themselves as a "congregation" and dubbed themselves and their island "Friendship." Octavio Ortiz would eventually have the chance to speak directly over his HAM radio with one "Ariel," one of the strange members of the Friendship.

In an interview with Spanish journalist and broadcaster Josep Guijarro, Ortiz explained that whenever Ariel speaks to him over the HAM radio, the needles on his equipment jump, indicating that a transmitter of enormous power is being employed. Nor is Ortiz the only one to speak with this entity: his wife, Cristina, boldly asked Ariel where he and his group came from. The voice replied that they were "not of this world, but belonged to Humankind."

In August 1985, little over a year since Ortiz relayed the message from the vessel besieged by the strange craft, a shining object appeared in the early afternoon over their home in Santiago. According to their testimony, a voice on the HAM radio bade them to "Come out! Come out!" After doing so and talking to Ariel on the HAM radio, they realized that the UFO was an object remotely controlled by the mysterious Friendship.

According to Guijarro, renowned ufologist Jorge E. Anfruns made note of a highly important detail: "Some of the HAM operators were phoning the newspapers to report interference with their sophisticated equipment."

Is this proof that a strange cabal actually controlled the saucer? The Ortiz family believes that the object was not remotely controlled, but that their friend Ariel was actually aboard it. More could be said about this bizarre sect of humans who possess advanced technology or aliens who claim some sort of kinship with our species, but it goes far beyond the scope of this writing. Suffice it to say that the Chilean Navy appears to have been aware for many years of the radio interference and problems caused by the strange objects operating in the vicinity of the Chonos islands. Josep Guijarro received a letter from a man who served five years at a naval radio station in Puerto Montt, stating: "We were sick of these devils, who often jammed our communications with immensely powerful high-tech distorting equipment, which on occasions even produced invisible barriers surrounding all of the Taitao Peninsula and left all boats, including the Navy, bereft of communications."

Delving further into the highly complex Friendship situation takes us away from the original issue: Are nonhumans presently reaching out to a Mexican "contactee" through radio, as Professor Cid's report suggests? Until further information is received from Rafael Oceguera, who is currently researching and documenting the case, this question remains open.

CHARACTERISTICS

MESSAGE TYPE: RADIO

FREQUENCY: MULTIPLE

OTHER PHENOMENA: YES (AS PART OF SIGHTINGS AND UFO PHENOMENA)

FROM: EXTRATERRESTRIAL

WITNESSES: YES (NUMEROUS HAM RADIO OPERATORS AND OTHERS)

ELEMENTS: INTERFERENCE AND MESSAGES.

Colin Andrews Shares a Personal Encounter

With new equipment, he recorded the TV presenters. The voice and picture disappeared and were replaced by a metallic voice for six full minutes. Colin recorded the entire event live. The broadcast was witnessed by two million people watching the news that evening. Within days, the area became the center of UFO and crop circle activity for the next forty years.

A message sample: "Be still now and listen, for your chance may not come again. You have a short time to live in peace and good will. You must learn to be sensitive to the voice within that can tell you what is truth and what is confusion, chaos, and untruth."

Andrews published the entire message—audio and video that he had recorded.

Colin had several experiences where simple thoughts in his mind about crop circles would then appear in the area, as if a message in response to his thought requests.

This silent request-and-answer message play has been reported independently by other experiencers as well. Colin believes it is the quantum energy field.

He explained, "Each person who has experienced a high strangeness event holds a small piece of a larger picture, and it's time to put these pieces together."

CHARACTERISTICS

MESSAGE TYPE: TELEVISION (BROADCAST INTERRUPTION)

FREQUENCY: ONCE

OTHER PHENOMENA: YES (AS PART OF UFO PHENOMENA AND OTHER INTERACTIONS)

FROM: EXTRATERRESTRIAL

WITNESSES: YES (THE BROADCAST WENT OUT TO TWO MILLION PEOPLE ON THE EVENING NEWS)

ELEMENTS: BROADCASTED MESSAGE. SOURCE NEVER FOUND NOR COULD BE TRACED.

MIB, Women in Black, and Phone Calls of the Sinister Kind
by Nick Redfern

Just about everyone has heard of the Men in Black. They are secret agents of an equally secret agency of government, right? They are the 007s of ufology, correct? No. Wrong on both counts. The idea that the MIB are employed by the likes of the CIA, the FBI, and the NSA is largely driven by the phenomenally successful Men in Black movie trilogy starring Will Smith and Tommy Lee Jones. In the movies, yes, the Men in Black *are* agents of government. But that's because the Smith and Jones productions were specifically based upon a short-lived comic-book series form the 1990s called—what else?—*The Men in Black*. It was the work of Lowell Cunningham and ran for just six issues. In Cunningham's stories, the MIB are regular guys with extraordinary jobs: They silence witnesses to UFOs and do their utmost to keep hostile aliens at bay. All of this is a very far cry from what most witnesses to the MIB actually report.

In the real world, the Men in Black—as well as the lesser-known Women in Black—are bone-chilling in appearance and nature. They are pale-faced, cadaverous ghouls who typically come out at night and force their ways into the homes of terrified UFO witnesses. They often use mind-control to get the information they need from those they target. People speak of falling sick after a visit from the WIB and the MIB, as if being in their malevolent presence can provoke a kind of "supernatural infection." Others have reported violent poltergeist activity in the family home after an ominous visit from the black-garbed fiends. Whatever the MIB are, the very *last* place they come from is the government. Theories for who or what the *real* Men in Black might be include tulpas, time-travelers, and demonic entities.

Nick Redfern Shares a Personal Encounter

In 2015, I spoke at the annual Contact in the Desert conference, which is held at Joshua Tree, California. I chose to speak on one of my areas of particular interest: the UFO "contactee" movement of the 1950s onward. Many of the tales of the contactees were undeniably outrageous, with witnesses claiming encounters with long-haired aliens and hot-looking space-babes. Yes, the tales are controversial in the extreme, but as a slab of 1950s-era Americana they are almost unbeatable.

One of the cases I spoke about at Joshua Tree concerned a woman whose story appears in the pages of none other than the now-declassified FBI file on the terrible tragedy of January 1986, when NASA's *Challenger* space shuttle exploded shortly after takeoff, killing all of the crew. In the immediate wake of the disaster, the FBI launched a number of investigations in response to claims that terrorists might have been the cause.

The woman in question—whose name is deleted from the FBI's papers—claimed to have been in contact with human-like alien beings who told her that, yes, *Challenger* was indeed sabotaged—by a powerful group of terrorists. The FBI was not used to dealing with such an unusual interviewee, but they faithfully recorded every word she had to say. I decided to make a mention of this strange story in my presentation at Contact in the Desert. And to provide the audience with something visual, I went online and downloaded a couple of photos of the *Challenger* and inserted them into my PowerPoint presentation.

A few hours after doing that, I phoned my literary agent, Lisa Hagan, on a completely different topic. During the conversation, though, Lisa told me that something very weird had happened just a couple of hours earlier. As I listened, Lisa told me that her phone rang and the phone's caller ID registered "Private Caller." Lisa said "Hello" and got a two-word reply: "*Challenger* exploded." The phone then went dead. Lisa is one hour ahead of me, time-wise, and when we checked, we found that Lisa received the call right around the time I was searching for a couple of pictures to illustrate my lecture. Both of us felt—and continue to feel—that someone was keeping tabs on both of us. Who? That's the big question that, so far, we have no answer to. But it's undeniably a classic example of how UFO researchers find themselves mixed up in the weird world of telephone interference, strange calls, and even stranger characters at the other end.

CHARACTERISTICS

MESSAGE TYPE: LANDLINE PHONE

FREQUENCY: ONCE

OTHER PHENOMENA: NO

FROM: EXTRATERRESTRIAL, UNKNOWN ENTITY

WITNESSES: NO

ELEMENTS: TIMING OF CALL AND SUBSTANCE OF MESSAGE COINCIDING WITH NICK'S IMAGE SEARCH.

I could go on and on with at least fifteen or twenty equally bizarre stories similar to those described above. But, by now, you get the point: when you immerse yourself in the UFO subject, don't be at all surprised if, late one dark and cold night, you find yourself on the receiving end of a menacing call from an equally menacing character.

About Nick Redfern

Nick Redfern is the author of many books, including *The Slenderman Mysteries, The Real Men in Black,* and *Women in Black.* He can be contacted at his blog, "World of Whatever," at *http://nickredfernfortean.blogspot.com.*

More on the Mothman Prophecies
John Keel
Point Pleasant, West Virginia, 1966

The following story comes from the archives of John Keel, of *The Mothman Prophecies* fame. It dates back to the mid-to-late 1960s when Keel spent a great deal of time in Point Pleasant, West Virginia, seeking out the truth of the fiery-eyed, winged monster of the book's title. Keel revealed a startling story:

A blond woman in her thirties, well-groomed, with a soft Southern accent, visited people in Ohio and West Virginia whom I had interviewed. She introduced herself as "John Keel's secretary," thus winning instant admission. The clipboard she carried held a complicated form filled with personal questions about the witnesses' health, income, the type of cars they owned, their general family background, and some fairly sophisticated questions about their

UFO sightings. Not the type of questions a run-of-the-mill UFO buff would ask. I have no secretary. I didn't learn about this woman until months later when one of my friends in Ohio wrote to me and happened to mention, "As I told your secretary when she was here. . . ." Then I checked and found out she had visited many people, most of whom I had never mentioned in print. How had she located them?

The mysterious woman didn't just visit those who had strange encounters in Point Pleasant and in some of the other nearby towns. She also phoned them, often at late hours. They were calls that were almost overwhelmed by static and probing questions. The mystery was never solved.

CHARACTERISTICS

MESSAGE TYPE: LANDLINE PHONE

FREQUENCY: MULTIPLE

OTHER PHENOMENA: YES

FROM: EXTRATERRESTRIAL, UNKNOWN ENTITY

WITNESSES: YES

ELEMENTS: PROBING QUESTIONS, STATIC.

Curious Entity Joins the Call
Brad Steiger
Ohio, 1968

In the late 1960s, there was a very weird affair that was shared with long-time researcher Brad Steiger, who shared the details with me. The incident was focused on a young UFO sleuth whom Steiger referred to as "Dan O." On the evening of July 13, 1968, Dan was chatting on the phone with a friend and colleague in the UFO field. Then, quite out of the blue, something very strange happened: Dan was suddenly interrupted by a woman. Steiger was told by Dan that "the third party identified herself as a Mrs. Slago, who, as she said, was accidentally connected with our line. She had been listening to our conversation strictly out of curiosity."

Although Dan and his colleague had no idea who the woman was, they actually continued the conversation—and made her a part of it. At first, it all sounded genial, and the woman sounded very intrigued and interested by what the pair had to say to her about alien life and flying saucers. That fairly genial atmosphere soon evaporated, however. Mrs. Slago soon suggested it would be a good idea—in fact, a very good idea—if they left the UFO subject alone and walked away from it. There was a clear threat in the woman's words.

Dan added: "She stated that UFO organizations should not attempt to further the investigation and study of UFOs, because as she put it, 'Earth people do not understand.' She stopped short of what she was about to say, as if she caught herself about to say something I should not hear."

Mrs. Slago then revealed that her real name was Nelson and she was in the employ of the local police. And then, oddly, she hung up. Checks by Dan revealed that there was no one by the name of Nelson or Slago with the local police, which is hardly surprising. The affair disturbed and worried Dan for days, which may have been the goal of the mysterious woman.

Dan's last words on the matter: "We had a complete check made on our telephone lines, but the check revealed no evidence of wire-tapping or anything of that sort. A check with the telephone company revealed that a misconnection of this type could not possibly have been made."

CHARACTERISTICS

MESSAGE TYPE: LANDLINE PHONE

FREQUENCY: MULTIPLE

OTHER PHENOMENA: YES

FROM: EXTRATERRESTRIAL, UNKNOWN ENTITY

WITNESSES: YES

ELEMENTS: CEASE AND DESIST ON UFO RESEARCH, STATIC, ENTITY JOINING THE CALL.

Call Interference from the Men in Black
Claudia Cunningham
New York, late 1970s

Claudia Cunningham of New York is someone whom I have come to know over the last few years. She is also someone who has had more than a few strange run-ins with the sinister Men in Black. One day, I hope, Claudia will write her very own book on her experiences. But until then, let's take a look at one of Claudia's strangest experiences.

In the late 1970s, I was married and my husband was a police officer who worked nights. Being alone and bored a lot, I was heavily into reading of the paranormal through my massive little library—and I was then reading *Phone Calls from the Dead* by Scott Rogo. The gist was that when someone died, they could call you, and the book gave many instances of this happening.

One night, I was in bed reading the book, and I snapped on the AM radio on my night table, and the show was WGY's talk show and they were interviewing UFO abductee Betty Hill. She said she had a lot of phone interference after seeing the UFO with her husband Barney—static, that sort of thing. I was very nervous that night listening to it and imagining my phone would ring. Imagine my shock when it *did* ring. This must have been around 9 p.m. at night...and all I could hear was static! Like I said, I was heavily into reading anything about UFOs, Bermuda Triangle, etc., and I think my fear triggered the call. I mean, I think fear attracts these entities and they were having, as John Lennon would say, "a larf" on yours truly.

CHARACTERISTICS

MESSAGE TYPE: LANDLINE PHONE

FREQUENCY: TWICE

OTHER PHENOMENA: YES

FROM: EXTRATERRESTRIAL, UNKNOWN ENTITY

WITNESSES: YES

ELEMENTS: CALL LINE INTERRUPTION, STATIC.

The Call that Never Happened
Nick Redfern
United Kingdom, 1980s

There is a story that was told to me by a good friend in the field of paranormal research, Neil Arnold. A prolific author, Neil's books include *Shadows in the Sky, Monster!,* and *Shadows on the Sea.* Neil relayed to me an undeniably creepy story that revolves around a Man in Black and a telephone.

I have a relative who in the 1980s saw a UFO and went to the local phone box to report it to the newspaper. As soon as he entered the phone box, a man appeared by the phone box and was staring in rather menacingly. My relative thought the man wanted to use the phone, so he motioned he wouldn't be long, but the man still stared. The man wore a dark suit. My relative came off the phone and said to the man: "You can use it now." But he just stood there. My relative told the newspaper that he would go to their offices to tell them of the sighting, but as soon as he got on the bus, he got a shocking headache. He thought he was going to pass out but persisted, but when he got to the office, no one working there knew what he was on about, and they all said they hadn't received a call from him.

CHARACTERISTICS

MESSAGE TYPE: LANDLINE PHONE (OUTGOING)

FREQUENCY: ONCE

OTHER PHENOMENA: YES (STRANGE PERSON)

FROM: EXTRATERRESTRIAL, UNKNOWN ENTITY

WITNESSES: NO

ELEMENTS: OUTGOING CALL NEVER RECEIVED AT THE OFFICE. TIME SLIP?

8

Case Characteristics and Data

*I'm terrified of the supernatural things, which is why I'm very grateful
that I don't see things like that. Because if I did see things of the paranormal
persuasion, I don't think I'd be able to continue making scary movies.*
—James Wan

We gathered up our featured case files to present what the data looks like as a whole. This includes cases classified as potentially real phenomena. Note that these insights do not necessarily represent the spread of the numbers across all possible cases. However, we can glean insight by looking at what these messages tell us as a whole, and we will offer comments on important observations within the data.

Total Case Files: 59

Geography:
Bavaria
England
Germany
Netherlands
California
Canada
Connecticut
Georgia
Indiana

Louisiana
Massachusetts
Michigan
Missouri
New York
Ohio
Pennsylvania
Texas
Utah
West Virginia

Message Type:

22 landline phone(s)
10 cell phone calls/texts
10 radio (all types)
7 computer
5 voice mail (includes answering machines)
4 television
3 speaker
2 cable box
2 letter

Other: Audio photo frame, magnetic doodle board, recording equipment, sneakers with lights (see Bonus Case 4 starting on page 201).

Note: Eight of these communicated using more than one medium.

Frequency:

30 multiple (3+): 51%
21 once: 36%
8 twice: 13%

These numbers discount all phantom messages as wrong numbers or hallucinations that don't support the data when approximately half of the cases we examined closely have multiple occurrences.

Other Phenomena:

32 yes: 54%

27 no: 46%

Cases with no other phenomena would be the most suspect for misinterpretation anomalies. However, if the message substance adds a layer of verification, then those cases increase our level of confidence that actual phenomena is being reported.

From:

22 unknown entities

13 extraterrestrial

5 mom

5 dad

4 grandma

2 brother

2 friend

2 uncle

2 stranger

1 grandpa

1 husband

1 wife

Note that more than one contact can be present in a case. In the category of unknown entities specifically, it was important for us to look for other elements that made these cases more likely to be unexplainable versus interference. Additional synchronicities make all the difference when the source is unidentifiable.

Witnesses:

42 yes: 71%

17 no: 29%

Witnesses can be argued are not definitive evidence. However, the insight that witnesses give is that the phenomena cannot be easily dismissed as hallucination or simple misinterpretation when you have others that experienced the same event(s). If you believe the witnesses, and we found none that even hinted of not being truthful, then additional insight can be gained.

Message Elements:

6 saying hello
5 no number displayed or traceable
3 disconnected
7 warning (to help or threaten)
3 predicting future
2 help

A Few Additional Elements of Interest:

Long-distance phone calls, some operator assisted in the old days, originated from phantom sources.

There was no record with the phone company.

Although rare, some contacts and messages can be quite long.

Calling on or related to time of death.

Static and third entity joins a call.

9

THEORIES AND DISCUSSION

Many a trip continues long after movement in time and space have ceased.
—John Steinbeck

One theory for the increase in these types of experiences is the fact that we have so many signals and electricity being used to power our world. Cell phones and cell phone towers appear to have increased the frequency of this phenomena, or at least expanded the overall universe of contact modalities. Therefore, the result is an increase in overall connectivity, utilization, and the resulting prevalence of unexpected contact. Other times, the more significant enabler of this phenomena is the manifestation of a larger haunting or paranormal flap area. This would be more conducive to a myriad of phenomena—UFO phenomena, cryptids, ghosts, or conceivably multiverse entities—both familiar ones as well as those that are of an uncertain or unknown origin. Phantom messages are possible without even knowing how to use the method of communication. Another assumption is that it takes a lot of energy for these communications to occur. Due to the use of energy and frequency, that theory makes sense, but it remains an absent element in a significant number of cases examined.

Electronics are either utilized when plugged in as normal, or the phenomena happens when the items are unplugged. Our investigation yields that the frequency for plugged in versus unplugged is roughly the same for each.

In the *American Horror Story* season entitled "Hotel" a vampire saves a character's father, but his Alzheimer's is still there, it just stopped progressing. If you do continue after death, do you retain your autism? Your Alzheimer's? We have not found any cases that involve messages from those with debilitating mental illness, only entities or those who claim to be notoriously wicked people when alive.

Psychologist Dr. Laurene M. Gomez summed it up nicely:

> I think what makes phantom messages so baffling is that we don't understand them, where they come from, how they are generated, and the motivational force behind them. We always seem to be drawn to that which we do not understand and cannot replicate upon command. We wonder why some folks are recipients of these messages and not others, or why they are not more commonplace rather than "odd phenomena." Just as with any means of communication, one has to be open to hearing the message if they wish to receive the information.

Kadrolsha Ona Carole, referred to as "Queen of the Paranormal," is a leading practitioner of energy healing, spirit communication, and the paranormal. She is the creator of the The Paranormal Hall of Fame. She told us:

> I am a firm believer that energy—a ghost—does not always come out and say "boo" on command. Many times, communication is uninvited. Personally, I love to conduct energy experiments at the large pop-culture conventions I appear at. My reasoning is this: Energy is like a magnet to bring forth more energy. The more energy in the room, the easier it is for me to help people communicate with the spirit world.

We have divided our theories and discussion categories into five sections:

1. Lack of understanding electronics.
2. Bereavement.
3. Our faulty memories.
4. Trickery: intentional and unintentional.
5. The paranormal.

1. Lack of Understanding Electronics

Delayed text or phone messages

Cell phone problems sometimes delay text messages from being received. At times, they can even arrive days later. If a loved one happened to die or have an accident between one of these delayed texts, it would appear as if a deceased person sent the messages. Unless it was the first time your phone delayed a message, you would likely be aware of the phone's issue. Even so, these delays can cause confusion, arguments, and important missed messages until they are fixed or the phone replaced.

Messages or calls with the number displaying all zeros

People often interpret this as a number that doesn't exist and therefore is from *somewhere* else. However, phantom messages most often come from known phone numbers or no display at all, rather than from the confusing display of all zeros. The origin of these calls can be Skype calls, out-of-country calls, blocked calls, or even calls from unassigned numbers. An unassigned number can also mean that the number is blocked; it does not mean the number doesn't exist and therefore is paranormal in nature. If these calls occur in conjunction with a meaningful event, then it's possible to make a false correlation of the call to that event, when no real causation or meaning exists.

Insects and rodents

The influence of insects and rodents should not be overlooked or underestimated. Both can cause interesting anomalies in photographs and make electronics behave in strange unexpected ways. Again, when these experiences correlate with significant emotional events, they can leave powerful impressions on the people experiencing the results.

Bill had a case in the 1980s during which the family security system alarm went off unexpectedly without any apparent reason. The grandmother, who was living with the family, had died just three days prior. They felt that Grandma was trying to communicate with them as they went through the process of accepting her passing. They tried taking photographs and achieved spectacular results with weird distortions and orbs in the photos. In a disgusting way, the answer presented itself. They contacted the alarm company to address a system malfunction. The cause of the mysterious behavior of the alarm was roaches infesting the unit and setting it off by making the system work erratically. Once they were removed, the system worked correctly again, and the family was told that an exterminator would be needed to prevent this from occurring in the future.

The photos were simply the usual light reflections misinterpreted by the eyes of laypeople. These are often mistaken for the paranormal, especially if there are any other concurrent events taking place. The orbs were a combination of dust and a smudge on the camera lens. These incidents, submitted as evidence, often sound mysterious, especially if the family omits embarrassing details, such as an insect problem once they realize that is the root cause of the erratic behavior for the electronics.

Rodents can cause similar issues and can also cause photo reflections that look like a person or other unknown entity. All animals and insects should be considered and eliminated in phantom messages, even in cases where there is other known activity present.

2. Bereavement
Hallucinations

Hallucinations brought on by grief are quite common, but not often discussed openly. Sights, sounds, touches, smells, presence, and contact are all reported as part of legitimate bereavement hallucinations. Many people are unaware that hallucinations under grief or stress are quite common and a normal experience by sober, healthy, well-adjusted individuals. And feeling a deceased one's presence, especially during the mourning process is more the norm than the exception. A December 2008 *Scientific American* article by Vaughan Bell sums up bereavement hallucinations as follows:

> We often fall back on the cultural catch-all of the "ghost" while the reality is, in many ways, more profound. Our perception is so tuned to their presence that when they are not there to fill that gap, we unconsciously try to mold the world into what we have lived with for so long and so badly long for. Even reality is no match for our love.

To attempt eliminating the bereavement hallucinatory experience in favor of a paranormal experience, the time of the message, other witnesses, and voice mails or additional physical evidence go far to help us analyze experiences accurately.

Psychologist Dr. Laurene M. Gomez has a different view:

I believe this is based on a false premise of "bereavement hallucinations," to which I do not subscribe. I do not distinguish between them [hallucinations vs. the paranormal], as I believe that they are one in the same. Contacts can last as long as people remain open to receiving them. I have known people who have seen, heard, or received messages from loved ones all throughout their lives. Others have received them in various times of crisis, such as when a child is sick or when facing extreme fear, loss, or hardship. There are others who can ask for connection and receive it almost immediately.

3. Our Faulty Memories
Mistaken call times

We all have memory issues. Our perception of what we think happened in the past and what really happened gets mixed up over time. We often unconsciously distort how things happened. In other words, we lie to ourselves without knowing it. This is why our parents always told us that if you lie, you will end up believing your lies. It's true. This is due to our faulty memories. In fact, we all harbor false memories. In effect, part of our makeup is self-rewritten. People have often raised these questions when pondering the existence of an afterlife. Are your false memories corrected in the next life, or do all those experiences remain distorted or outright incorrect? Memory causes us to question our experiences and everyone—especially ourselves. A classic example is simply mistaking the time of a call so you think it is before the person died. We did not find a case where this is apparent, however, the possibility exists, so we looked to eliminate basic memory errors before going forward in the elimination process.

Reconstruction: Our perception versus reality

The art of magic depends upon our inability to accurately reconstruct in our minds what we experience when seeing a magic trick. What we perceive as happening is incorrect 100 percent of the time when magic is successfully executed. Our brain is also incorrect when tricked by optical illusions. But what happens when no one is trying to trick us? What if no one is trying to influence or direct our attention, thoughts, and interpretations of what we see or experience? We often fool ourselves through faulty reconstruction of our experiences. There are many reasons as to why this happens. We will explore the most significant ones.

The lack of knowledge is one hinderance to reconstruction. This can originate due to the lack of analytic skills, interest (being caught off guard), or even the lack of ability to apply imagination to the experience. UFO sightings are an example in which lack of knowledge can lead to specific reconstruction problems. Astronomers, for example, report UFOs less than non-astronomers. By eliminating astrological mistakes due to specialized knowledge, errors in interpretation of experiences are reduced.

The second problem with reconstruction is we reject explanations that seem implausible to us. Uncanny coincidences happen all the time and are just that: mathematically driven probability that we can choose to accept or reject for something else that we personally feel is more rewarding. Emotional impact of the experience adds to its ability to convince us it is more likely something meaningful, because it *feels* that way. A magician often depends on the obvious explanations being rejected by the observer, even though those might be the correct explanations after all.

Lastly, and a form of false memory, is faulty recall—misremembering. This innate human practice makes reconstruction to solve the puzzle impossible. This is due to the omission of some details and the addition or morphing of other details. It is important to realize that these errors are not intentional. They are errors in our perception and memory. As Elbert Hubbard once said, "A miracle: an event described by those to whom it was told by those who did not see it."

Throughout history, people have passed down stories incorrectly even when they were direct witnesses to the event. In magic, a great example of this is a spectator's attempt to reconstruct the details of an impossible feat of magic. Original witnesses of performances of the old Indian rope trick later would exaggerate what they originally saw. In fact, the trick started as a made-up experience, and magicians then decided to perform their own versions to make it a viewable reality.

The reconstructions of this trick with incorrect descriptions throughout the years have resulted in a miracle that even magicians cannot duplicate at a performance! The legend outgrew the actual demonstration. It is common for magicians to be credited with doing feats they never did in the way described. Note that these witnesses truly believe what they saw and believe they are retelling or reconstructing the details with surgical accuracy.

This is the most recognizable image of the Indian rope trick that spurred faulty witness testimony. The Great Karachi, a famous Indian magician, was not Indian at all. He was actually from the United Kingdom. His real name is Arthur Derbyh.

It's important to remember that not all events are reconstructed poorly or inaccurately. Additional witnesses or a quantity of experiences might support the paranormal hypothesis, but not always. This is something we always must be cognizant of and work hard at uncovering when trying to discover whether the paranormal should be considered.

4. Trickery: Intentional and Unintentional
Spoofing numbers
Disguising call origins, known as spoofing, is another technological item to consider. Hacking and other fraud falls under this subject as well.

Dead calling services
Although we did not find a specific instance of someone being haunted this way, services exist where people can pay to have timed messages sent to loved ones *after* their death. This can be seen as a cruel move or a comforting one. Either way, it's an added layer of difficulty in investigating these cases. Prerecorded voice messages, coupled with disguised origin of emails or text messages (or access given to accounts), can make for a very haunted, yet perhaps cruel and uncalled-for set of phantom messages. New phone apps are being introduced to send prepared timed messages after your death if you wish. So let's just say it's an evolving business model for morbid pranks. One thing we know is most grandmas are not using these services.

Harry Houdini in his own words: On fraud and our minds
Note: Houdini talks about Spiritualism because it was the predominant "paranormal" movement at the time.

If the wish be father to the thought, it is mother to the hallucination of the senses. The tricks the brain can play without calling in Spiritualistic aids are simply astounding, and only those who have made a study of morbid as well as normal psychology, realize the full truth of this.

Mine has not been an investigation of a few days or weeks or months, but one that has extended over thirty years. In that thirty years, I have not found one incident that savored of the genuine. If there had been any real unalloyed demonstration to work on, one that did not reek of fraud, one that could not be reproduced by earthly powers, then there would be something for a foundation, but up to the present time, everything I have investigated has been the result of deluded brains or those which were too actively and intensely willing to believe.

The startling feature has been the utter inability of the average human being to describe accurately anything he or she has witnessed. Many sitters, devoid of the sense of acute observation, prefer to garnish and embellish their stories with the fruits of their fertile imaginations, adding a choice bit every time the incident is reported, and eventually, by a trick of the brain, really believing what they say. It is evident, therefore, that by clever misguidance and apt misdirection of attention, a medium can accomplish seeming wonders. The sitter becomes positively self-deluded and actually thinks he has seen weird phantoms or has heard the voice of a beloved one. To my knowledge I have never been baffled in the least by what I have seen at seances. Everything I have seen has been merely a form of mystification. The secret of all such performances is to catch the mind off guard and the moment after it has been surprised to follow up with something else that carries the intelligence along with the performer, even against the spectator's will. When it is possible to do this with a highly developed mind like Mr. Kellar's, one trained in magic mystery, and when scientific men of the intelligence of Sir Oliver Lodge, Sir Arthur Conan Doyle, the late William Crookes and William T. Stead, can be made to believe by such means, how much easier it must be in the case of ordinary human beings. I cannot accept nor even comprehend the intelligence which justifies the conclusion, so often put in print as the opinion of brainy men supporting Spiritualism, that admits the possibility of a result being accomplished by natural means but nevertheless assert their sincere belief that the identical performance by a professional medium is solely of supernatural origin and guidance, nor can I understand the reasoning that, acknowledging the disreputable character of certain practitioners or mediums, deliberately defends the culprits in the performance of what has been proven a crime. Is it true logic, logic that would stand either in court or club room, to say that a medium caught cheating ninety-nine times out of a hundred was honest the hundredth time because not caught? Would the reader trust a servant who stole ninety-nine articles and then professed innocence when the hundredth article was missing?

Sir Conan Doyle asks in all innocence, "Is it really scientific to deny and at the same time refuse to investigate?"

My answer is most emphatically "no." Nevertheless, they absolutely oppose all honest efforts at investigation, and justify the mediums in refusing to work when the conditions are not just as they want them. When one is invited to a dark seance for the purpose of investigation and finds the conditions so fixed as to bar him from enquiring too closely and compel him to be content with merely looking on, he stands a poor chance of getting at the facts, and should he dare to disregard the "rules of the circle" and the seance results in a blank, the investigator is charged with having brought an atmosphere of incredulity to bear which prevents manifestation.

I do not affirm that the claims of Spiritualism are disproved by such failures, but I do say that if under such circumstances one dared to investigate properly and sanely, and to cross-examine, as he most certainly would do in any other form of investigation, scientific, or in the other walks of life, Spiritualism would not be so generously accepted.

In justification, the psychic says that darkness or excessively dim light is perfectly legitimate, and that tangible investigation might result in injury or even death to the medium. The folly of any such fear has been proven time and again by the unexpected play of a flash light. Even the ardent supporters who lay emphasis on such an absurdity have, according to their own confession, made, or had made, flashlight photographs and there has never been a single case of harm or disaster reported. This necessity for darkness seems but the grossest invention of the medium to divert, even to the point of intimidation, the attention of the sitters. Such a necessity cannot be accorded a logical reason for existing under test conditions to demonstrate a scientific subject. It can be supported only as a visionary, speculative superstition; an instrument to foster hallucinatory illusion and as an admirable subterfuge to cover fraud.

Note from the authors: We wish Houdini could have been on some poltergeist cases or other hauntings so he could have discovered something of merit. Understandably, since Spiritualism was the major force in the paranormal arena at that time, it made sense to pursue those practitioners. Unfortunately, it was not the route where he was going to find any genuine paranormal phenomena. Unlike other skeptics, who concluded without investigating, we can be proud that Houdini investigated intensely. His search for real magic was an admirable one.

5. The Paranormal
Psychokinesis manifestation

An older theory is that these phantom messages are not coming from other entities or loved ones or aliens, but they are manifestations caused by psychokinesis from the person receiving the messages. This doesn't fit well with the cases we've looked at, especially when these message experiences have witnesses and voicemails and other haunting phenomena in conjunction with them.

Bill: As a magician, I know of many techniques to cause psychokinetic demonstrations. I have never witnessed a person capable of a real demonstration no matter how confident the people were that referred me to them. The non-magician is simply not trained to be able to determine if the person is able to manifest actual phenomena of this sort. I am also not the one to determine when mental illness is the obvious cause. As Bill Roll always said, we must bring in the proper professionals to assist. Because of this, I have doubts of any manifestation of this type, but I am happy to change my viewpoint if proper evidence is ever forthcoming. So far, people-driven phenomena, like remote viewing and other spiritualism inventions, don't produce anything that would come close to qualify as unexplainable. That is not to say that, in conjunction with other haunting or phenomena, there might be other impacting drivers of the haunt. We must always be suspect; especially when the messages utilize an intermediary.

Actual communicating with the dead

Another theory is that you are actually getting messages from the dead.

Tony Spera on Phantom Messages

I believe that the deceased do communicate with us. It's just that we are kind of tuned out. I think they act as spirit guides—actually influencing our thoughts—trying to guide us in the right direction. They can manipulate electronic devices on Earth from their dimension. I believe electronic devices act as a kind of conduit, enabling spirits to communicate with us from the other side, and God allows this communication from spirits to loved ones to comfort those who really need the contact to get through the grieving process. The way it was portrayed in the movie *Ghost* is a good example. Spirits learn how to communicate, move objects, etc. Spirits need a means to make contact. After all, they no longer possess a physical body. Therefore, they manipulate other media, such as electronic devices to use them as voice boxes, because they no longer have vocal chords. As evidenced in the Enfield poltergeist case, the spirits used Margaret's and Janet's vocal chords to produce sound. That is called a materialized larynx. There are many mysteries of the universe. These communications are one of them, because we don't fully understand how spirits actually manipulate these devices to communicate with the living.

About Tony Spera

Tony is director of The New England Society for Psychic Research (NESPR). He is a paranormal researcher and the son-in-law of Ed and Lorraine Warren, who founded NESPR in 1952. Tony is former police officer with more than forty years of experience exploring the paranormal. He has appeared on numerous television programs and has lectured at many colleges and universities. Tony also served as a consultant for the movies *The Conjuring* and *The Conjuring 2* by New Line Cinema.

Part of a Larger Haunting: Poltergeist, Paranormal Flap Areas, and So On

These experiences become easier to justify as real phenomena when they occur as a part of an overall haunting or other paranormal manifestation. Although we still need to validate that it is part of those occurrences, it certainly provides us with more insight and potential versus the one-time incident that could be subject to multiple explanations outside of the paranormal.

Electromagnetic energy

We're pretty much all in agreement that the paranormal is enabled by electromagnetic energy. When asking entities known and unknown, they even confirm this—for whatever good that does. A phantom message asked about how the call could be possible, and the answer is the use of the electrical currents that are produced by the technology in question.

The multiverse

Why is the multiverse (or the idea of multiple universes) in the paranormal section? Fair question, but I think we do know why. The paranormal does not exist outside of science or nature; it is the undiscovered part of it. Everything was paranormal before we understood it. Remember when the gods delivered the thunder and lightning? It was paranormal until we understood meteorology.

And not long ago in the 1540s, Copernicus told us the Earth-centered universe does not explain the motion of planets well. In fact, it goes against what you are observing. That new realization, being the result of solid science, observation, and hard work, changed our understanding of the world.

We believe that science is catching up to the paranormal as it has always done. For most people, viruses and natural disasters are no longer curses, and epileptic seizures are no longer blamed on demons.

The multiverse is not an idea that scientists simply imagined after having a few beers and chatting. Quantum physics is not armchair philosophy or good science fiction writing. That's the big difference. Rather than making your own conclusion and forcing new knowledge and experience to fit those views, science followed the data, and the multiverse is where the data led them. Interpreting what the data tells us about the cosmos, however, is not a small undertaking. There no place for human bias here. That is evident by the reality that many physicists aren't fond of the idea of the multiverse. Opinions don't matter though. We must follow where the data leads and try to make sense of things from there.

Physicists took the data and developed theories of how multiple universes could work, based on what we know from quantum physics. The most popular theory is the one we will focus on, especially because what science is seriously considering would neatly explain what we see in the paranormal.

One of the best illustrations for this is still Schrödinger's Cat, a thought experiment created by Austrian physicist Erwin Schrödinger in 1935. It says that two quantum states can be added together to create a new one. Where does that idea come from? The famous double-slit experiment, where we are able to watch electron waves present different outcomes in this way. With Schrödinger's Cat, the idea is that when this quantum addition takes place, there will be a state where the cat is both alive and dead from being exposed to a broken flask of poison. The real outcome that you observe takes place when you look to see which state the cat is in. But that's in your universe. Even if the cat is dead when you look, it is alive in another universe. And these splits can go on forever, so the theory goes. This means Jimmy and I are loved by all women in one of these universes. It's a fact. Why? Because all possible realities exist, so that reality exists too.

What does this have to do with phantom messages? Fair question again. This popular "many worlds" theory of quantum mechanics means that all possible realities exist. We don't usually see any of them but the ones in our universe. For those of us that experience the paranormal, you might be getting a rare glimpse of alternate universes, where other possibilities exist. The many worlds sometimes come together like two bubbles joining. Old-timers would call this "the veil being thin." In other words, the separation between the universe we experience, and other universes, intersect. In quantum physics, other universes are not in faraway space. They exist in the same space we operate in. The result might be what led to us talking about the veil, the flap, the portal, the other dimension, and so on. In this theory, they all would be other names that refer to quantum supposition.

What are the implications of this? If we test the many worlds theory against quantum mechanics, the result is fascinating: In phantom message cases where one meant to call, never did, but the call and message was received anyway, we have Schrödinger's Cat. The pop term for this is the "butterfly effect," and many physicists agree it exists. Basically, this case is as expected if you somehow created two different realities: one that made the phone call, and one that didn't.

Ghosts or spirits that appear to be of the dead would be very much alive in the quantum multiverse. Without a doubt, cases where the living haunt the living (unbeknownst to themselves), mirrors incidents when we would assume the spirit is "dead," such as when Grandma makes an impossible call. Why do these parallel worlds intersect? I think we can all agree it is related to energy. Death, sending out negative frequencies (as in a poltergeist case), and murder are examples of frequencies that appear to impact the "many worlds." Lastly, entities unknown to us (other than through paranormal experiences) can also exist in these infinite universes.

We must also consider that the multiverse might not answer all paranormal questions. History has taught us there might be multiple causes. Bill thinks this is the best theory out there, but he wouldn't bet his life on it.

Luis Elizondo, a former Department of Defense intelligence official who oversaw the Pentagon's UFO program, revealed their best theory on UFOs' ability to appear, maneuver, and disappear can be summed up with "quantum entanglement," that is, the multiverse. This shocking 2017 disclosure of the secret program has renewed enthusiasts and serious researchers alike; perhaps we will see a bit of disclosure in the years that follow. At least we might be heading in the right direction.

A few examples of other current theories of the multiverse include universes located far outside our universe, black holes producing new universes similar to the parent universe, and the hologram universe concept, for example, aliens simulating universes and ourselves in it, for example, *The Matrix*.

10

The Next 100 Years: What Will We Know?

Life to me is a journey—you never know what may be your next destination.
—David Russell

There is one prediction we do know with certainty: We will not be able to fully picture what we will know, build, and solve in a hundred years. It won't be surprising if we have new questions that we are not asking now. Perhaps some of these questions involve what we *used* to call the paranormal that are now understood scientific realities. It's natural for us all to want answers and to want those answers now. Before committing to an answer, see where the data leads and be ready to change direction as you learn, as all great scientists have been forced to do throughout history.

What have we accomplished in the last hundred years? In the 20th century, we almost doubled our life expectancy. Upgrading the human body and mind is currently taking place with medical advances. In the future, broader applications of these capabilities could produce a world that resembles something found in the fiction section of your favorite Barnes and Noble bookstore.

We now have super abilities that are more powerful than the gods of years ago. Greek, Hindu, African, and even modern "living" gods fail to possess or use the ease of communication that most ten-year-olds now grip in their little growing hands: the cell phone. Instead of sending an animal as a messenger like some gods had to resort to, we can simply call direct anywhere in the world. And our agricultural techniques far outperform our ancestors, most lofty prayers for healthy harvests. *We are the only known species that changed the global ecology all by ourselves.* Ironically, we are even positioned to replace natural selection with intelligent design. All along the way, we believe that we know the truth and others believe in superstitions. New technologies kill old gods and give birth to new gods. That's why agricultural deities were different from hunter-gatherer spirits.

Some of our godly advances include the understanding of the weather, lightning bolts, thunder, fertility, agriculture, society structure, how to gain knowledge and determine truths, the fact that human and child sacrifices do not work, and what the sun and moon really are. The list of discoveries goes on and on.

We should be proud of how smart we are now. Still, it's impossible for us to see all of what we will discover in 100 years. To demonstrate an actual example of an attempt to predict our future predicament, we've included portions of an interesting article published back in the year 1900 that predicts what life will be like in the year 2000. You'll find it enchanting, especially the ones that predict digital photography (not specifically), our growing height and population, and a few others. You'll also be amazed at how we pictured our future world. Every 100 years that follow will be increasingly difficult to make predictions. The benefits of compounding knowledge will lead to new unexpected realities. How do you picture our next 100 years?

"What May Happen in the Next Hundred Years"
Ladies' Home Journal, December 1900
By John Elfreth Watkins Jr.

These prophecies will seem strange, almost impossible. Yet, they have come from the most learned and conservative minds in America. To the wisest and most careful men in our greatest institutions of science and learning I have gone, asking each in his turn to forecast for me what, in his opinion, will have been wrought in his own field of investigation before the dawn of 2001—a century from now. These opinions I have carefully transcribed.

The Next 100 Years: What Will We Know?

Prediction #1: 350,000,000 to 500,000,000 people in America.

Prediction #2: Americans will be taller by from one to two inches. He will live fifty years instead of thirty-five as at present—for he will reside in the suburbs.

Prediction #3: Exercise will be compulsory in the schools.

Prediction #4: All hurry traffic will be below or high above ground and teem with capacious automobile passenger coaches and freight with cushioned wheels.

Prediction #5: Trains will run two miles a minute, normally; express trains one hundred and fifty miles an hour. Cars will, like houses, be artificially cooled.

Prediction #6: Automobiles will have been substituted for every horse vehicle now known.

Prediction #7: There will be air-ships; they will be maintained as deadly war-vessels by all military nations. Some will transport people and goods.

Prediction #8: Aerial war-ships and forts on wheels. Giant guns will shoot twenty-five miles or more, and will hurl anywhere within such a radius shells exploding and destroying whole cities.

Prediction #9: Photographs will be telegraphed from any distance. If there be a battle in China a hundred years hence snapshots of its most striking events will be published in the newspapers an hour later.

Prediction #10: We will see around the world. Persons and things of all kinds will be brought within focus of cameras connected electrically with screens at opposite ends of circuits, thousands of miles at a span.

Prediction #11: No mosquitoes or flies.

Prediction #12: Peas as large as beets. Plants will be made proof against disease microbes just as readily as man is to-day against smallpox.

Prediction #13: Strawberries as large as apples will be eaten by our great-great-grandchildren for their Christmas dinners a hundred years hence. Melons, cherries, grapes, plums, apples, pears, peaches and all berries will be seedless.

Prediction #14: Roses will be as large as cabbage heads. It will be possible to grow any flower in any color and to transfer the perfume of a scented flower to another which is odorless.

Prediction #15: No foods will be exposed. Liquid-air refrigerators will keep great quantities of food fresh for long intervals.

Prediction #16: English will be a language of condensed words expressing condensed ideas.

Prediction #17: A university education will be free to every man and woman. Poor students will be given free board, free clothing, and free books if ambitious and actually unable to meet their school and college expenses.

Prediction #18: Wireless telephone and telegraph circuits will span the world. By an automatic signal they will connect with any circuit in their locality without the intervention of a "hello girl."

Prediction #19: Automatic instruments reproducing original airs exactly will bring the best music to the families of the untalented. Thus, will great bands and orchestras give long-distance concerts.

Prediction #20: Coal will not be used for heating or cooking. It will be scarce, but not entirely exhausted. We will have found electricity manufactured by waterpower to be much cheaper.

Prediction #21: Hot or cold air will be turned on from spigots to regulate the temperature of a house as we now turn on hot or cold water from spigots to regulate the temperature of the bath. Rising early to build the furnace fire will be a task of the olden times.

Prediction #22: Pneumatic tubes, instead of store wagons, will deliver packages and bundles.

Prediction #23: Ready-cooked meals will be bought from establishments similar to our bakeries of today. Food will be served hot or cold to private houses in pneumatic tubes or automobile wagons.

Prediction #24: Winter will be turned into summer and night into day by the farmer. In cold weather he will place heat-conducting electric wires under the soil of his garden and thus warm his growing plants. He will also grow large gardens under glass.

Prediction #25: Fast-flying refrigerators on land and sea will bring delicious fruits from the tropics and southern temperate zone within a few days.

Prediction #26: Few drugs will be swallowed or taken into the stomach unless needed for the direct treatment of that organ itself. Not only will it be possible for a physician to actually see a living, throbbing heart inside the chest, but he will be able to magnify and photograph any part of it. This work will be done with rays of invisible light.

Prediction #27: There will be no wild animals except in menageries. Rats and mice will have been exterminated. Food animals will be bred to expend practically all of their life energy in producing meat, milk, wool, and other by-products.

Prediction #29: Fast electric ships, crossing the ocean at more than a mile a minute, will go from New York to Liverpool in two days.

Even though they came close on some predictions, there are far-reaching implications of the tools that would accomplish these fantastic feats. How could they have imagined the cell phone? Sure, Tesla did, but for the rest of us, it's a magical box some of us had to do without when we were growing up. And as amazing as it is, we complain when it's slow. Video games? Virtual reality? Programming capabilities? 3D printers? Laser surgery? The list can go on and on. We can guess at our next hundred years and the miracles they will bring, but some of the discoveries we will have trouble imaging. Of course, there might be a few Teslas out there to help speed things along.

EPILOGUE

Phantom messages are versatile. They don't go away as landline usage decreases or as society gravitates toward cellular and alternate forms of communication. Instead, phantom messages thrive as landline to landline, cell phone to landline, and cell phone to cell phone. They can involve electronics built into sneakers, the delivering of custom letters, and even cable boxes. As cable boxes go away, it doesn't matter. They show themselves on television and computers. They even search the Internet.

Inexplicable contacts continue within a constantly progressing environment. From Morse code to potential signals from outer space, modality will transform, but phantom messages are not going away.

—William J. Hall and Jimmy Petonito

P.S. Enjoy the bonus section! We wanted to share a few interesting cases with you. Thanks!

SECTION 2

BONUS CASES

CASE 1

THE ANGRY HOUSE

I will never step foot in that house again.
—Sandra Reyford, homeowner

Investigated by Shane Sirois and Bill Hall

Sandy's husband passed away on October 29, 2013. She told Bill she thought she was going crazy from what happened to her.

You see, they saw things—unexplainable things—in that house. And she refused to ever step inside again. The house is in Bridgeport, Connecticut, not far from the infamous Bridgeport Poltergeist house on Lindley Street (the subject of Bill's first book).

Her husband, Charles, had a nephew who was a police officer at the time of the Lindley Street incident. Charles told Sandy that his nephew said to believe what you hear and see because he was in there and saw the impossible happen. His superior told the officers not to speak about what they witnessed. That led Sandy to reach out to Bill.

Sandy had a Hartford Insurance adjuster come to inspect the foundation to see if they had a foundation problem. United Illuminating checked the electrical too. Until then, she had no thoughts that something more sinister was to blame.

She contacted a paranormal group who came to the house. The couple had a difficult time staying. It was not uncommon for them to leave and stay at a hotel.

Due to Sandy's husband's failing health, a private firm was hired to watch the house when she was away. She didn't tell them about her experiences there. Soon after, she received a distress call from the lead agent.

He was in a heightened state because the agent on duty that night called and in a panic pleaded, "I saw something. I really did. And I refuse to ever go back into that house."

The insurance adjuster came to inspect the house and stopped short before entering. She made the sign of the cross. Talking in a shrill voice she said, "Sandy, please don't leave me alone."

Back outside the house, the adjuster stood at the curb, hugging herself tightly while shivering and looking back up toward the house. She kept shaking her head and said firmly, "I don't want to be in that house, and you should not be in there either. I have been in many houses, and in this one I felt instantly that there is something wrong."

Sandy just wanted confirmation that "something" was in there. After all, she hadn't stepped foot in that house since July 2014. At times, she would go to open the door to let various people in, but Sandy always stopped short of entering. The top stoop to open the door was the farthest she would venture under any condition.

One time when she was still living there, her son-in-law entered the house. Sandy describes him as kind and gentle. Not this night. He entered the evil house and he transformed. As his eyes widened, he walked over to a corner of the basement and picked up a sledge hammer. He then wandered around speaking, but it was inaudible.

Sandy's sister and Sandy yelled, "Stop! Stop! Tony, stop it!" Sandy said her daughter did not want him back in that house. When Shane and Bill investigated the house, they found holes in the walls, courtesy of the sledgehammer. That was Tony's first time in the basement, and his last. He also made the sign of the cross before first entering the house.

This house was haunted. Sandy was sure of it. It had cold spots. At times, grey hues filled the house. Charles even carried on complete conversations to someone or something that she couldn't see.

"Outside the house, Charles was fine," Sandy explains.

Sandy provided in-depth details to Shane and Bill about this angry house. Contractors, property managers, and others that entered the house questioned Sandy about whether she heard or saw strange things in there.

"Life was difficult though," Sandy explained. "We fought constantly and blamed each other. For the lights on in the basement, Charles thought I was stealing his jewelry since it was mysteriously disappearing." Other elements noted include:

- Footsteps from heavy, hard-soled shoes.
- Scratches on Sandy's chest and left arm.
- Basement lights turning themselves on.
- The alarm clock would not shut off no matter what Charles did. He finally cut the wires to make it turn off. The ADT house alarm went off, but ADT had no record of the occurrence.
- Bedroom door handle jiggling, knocks on the door.
- Whispers heard by multiple people.
- Strange circles caught on their security cameras.
- Chairs shaking violently while Sandy and Charles were sitting in them.
- Smell of rotten milk.
- Charles described what looked like a swarm of bees in technicolor above Sandy's head.
- Light switches refused to turn off the lights.

Shane Sirois and Bill Hall Investigate

Shane and I met Sandy at the abandoned alleged haunted house. We all walked up the lawn and stopped at the stoop to the side door.

Sandy reiterated the rules, "I'll unlock this door but leave it closed. Then, I'll walk back to my car. Don't open the door until I am down these steps."

She clearly didn't want any chance of even peeking inside that horrifying house. Shane went back to his truck for some supplies while I entered the side door right into the kitchen. There were no tables or chairs, just a single wheelchair. I, of course, sat down. Shane came back and now we were better able to light the way so we could look around. Shane didn't feel anything there. He has a sense for the presence of the paranormal.

We walked room to room and nothing. We saw holes in a few walls from the sledgehammer that Tony used when his personality changed in the angry house. We also saw the property management crew's labels, parts, and tools strewn around like they abandoned their project and never came back, which is exactly what they did. They went there and worked and soon let Sandy know that they quit, and she knew why.

It was time to check out the basement. Shane and I headed down. Our eyes focused instantly when we found the sledgehammer. It was still stuck in the finished wall in a hole it made. Stuck there like the event was frozen in time. There were holes everywhere. A nice lattice basement door was crushed in and broken. Pieces were on the floor like a crime scene that was left untouched since the night it happened. There was a pile of miscellaneous storage items around and even Christmas presents, which remained unwrapped and never to be recovered again.

Shane still felt nothing. We found clean portable folding chairs so we sat down to close our eyes and be still to see if we could experience anything. First, we talked a bit, and I noticed a partially unwrapped Christmas present that was a case of beer. Knowing Sandy didn't want anything in that house, or at least the beer, we had a beer. It was very convenient. And it wasn't even gift time. Still nothing.

We returned to the house with Shane armed to check out the EMF in the home to see if that could be causing some of the issues, particularly the change in personalities.

Shane enters the house. *Photo by Bill Hall.*

The basement wall with a sledgehammer stuck in it. *Photo by Bill Hall.*

The destroyed basement door lattice. Shane investigates the other side of the basement. *Photo by Bill Hall.*

Shane's Assessment

During the two visits, my assessment remained unchanged. There was no entity or presence in the home. Negative parasitic entities do not haunt homes. They haunt people. With the home empty, entities almost never stick around. I'm not saying that there couldn't have been one before. Even with it gone, it does not mean the house is okay. It is not.

What we found can cause more harm, both mentally and physically, than most entities, but not all. An explanation of what we found follows. Even with the electricity turned off, there was still a very high electromagnetic field (EMF) in that house, especially in the kitchen and in the corner of the basement directly under the kitchen. I suspect the paranormal group you had there might have attributed that to a ghost or negative entity—but it's neither of the two.

Even when the power is turned off to the house, EMF is still present. The kitchen and basement spots I mentioned are near an access panel in the basement. I opened it and found the ground cable coming in from the ground rod outside. Every home has a ground rod that is inserted in the ground, and the cable will attach to the electrical ground wiring and the metal and/or copper piping. This is so if your home gets hit by lightning, it will go into the ground. I placed my EMF meter close to this wire and it maxed the meter's reading out at over 200.0 milligauss. A healthy home should read no higher than .3 inside a living area. It's okay for it to be high around refrigerators, microwaves, or other electronics. However, there is a substantial amount of EMF coming in from Sandy's ground cable.

High EMF such as this can cause paranoia, anger, feeling you're being watched, rage, headaches, dizziness, shadowy movements in your peripheral, shadow figures in your direct line of vision (usually grey or greenish), ocular migraines (psychedelic color patterns in direct line of vision), depression, psycho-sexual disorders, lowered immune system, and even cancer (most often tumors in adults and leukemia in children).

There are two types of EMFs: ionizing and nonionizing. Ionizing EMF is the most damaging. Nonionizing at lower readings doesn't seem to pose a threat. This is most common in homes. Even nonionizing EMF is known to destroy melatonin, which suppresses the mutation of cells and cancerous tumor growths, in addition to aiding in sleep. I believe this is responsible for everything in that house. It triggers fear in almost every person. They run machines that produce 33 hz at scary attractions so the audience will already be in the mood before entering. It has also been shown in laboratory studies to make objects move, doors to open and close, and humans to go out of their minds with fear. This is all proven by science.

The effects of EMF can also be responsible for creating the state of being in people that will attract a parasitic entity. Sandy may or may not have had one at some time in that house. It is not there any longer.

About Shane Sirois

Shane Sirois has been helping individuals and families afflicted by the paranormal for more than thirty years. As of this printing, his success rate of dispelling negative entities remains at 100 percent due to understanding paranormal mechanics.

Shane is a shaman, which Bill Hall would have rolled his eyes at and said was "woo woo" if he had not seen Shane's talents firsthand during their investigation detailed in Bill's second book, *The Haunted House Diaries*.

Shane's Approach to the Paranormal

Shane uses a strict scientific process, along with advanced understanding of how to diagnose and treat any disturbance in any home. He never uses religion, noting that you need to directly address the root cause of the parasite. When religion works, it's not for the reason people think. It can temporarily change your thinking, but inevitably, the disturbances return. These parasites never subscribed to any of the gods throughout history.

CASE 2

A Black-Winged Shadow Creature and Top Hat Man

The only thing that permits human beings to collaborate with one another in a truly open-ended way is their willingness to have their beliefs modified by new facts. Only openness to evidence and argument will secure a common world for us.
—Sam Harris

Investigated by Bill Hall, with Shane Sirois

My friend Jill texted me and asked if I could help Amy. She has suffered through encounters with a black-winged shadow creature for five long years. As a matter of protocol, I had to eliminate other potential causes of seeing a shadow figure. Was she suffering from sleep paralysis, where people can see a shadowy figure approaching them as they lie paralyzed and become increasingly alarmed? In other words, a very real hallucination? If you are half awake in an unbalanced emotional state, natural paranoia might set in, causing an ordinary shadow to look alive, or it could be a hypnogogic perception; this is where that old sweater thrown over the chair at the far end of the room suddenly looks like a monster peering right at you and starting to move toward you. Once awake, it returns to be the old stupid sweater you forgot about. Lastly, methamphetamine abuse must be ruled out. Addicts often experience shadow people, especially after long bouts of sleep deprivation. These hallucinations will stand in doorways, walk behind you, or come at you on the sidewalk. They are written about throughout the ages in our folklore, at a time when all experiences were real because we had no knowledge of how vivid hallucinations can be.

Amy didn't fit any of these ordinary explanations for her sightings of the infamous black-winged shadow creature, known to be a highly dangerous archetype as a paranormal parasite. What are they? A negative entity, yes. Although I hate to classify entities as all or nothing. If they are anything like us, they will be "somewhere on the spectrum," as they say.

Many black-winged shadow creature encounters happen when in bed, waking, and seeing them at the door. As we discussed, these circumstances must be examined closely to eliminate sleep paralysis. In cases of real phenomena, the entity is a solid three-dimensional figure. It doesn't simply move or waver like with a hallucination. Instead, it lifts its arms up as its huge wings expand. That's the tipping point when the victim is now fully awake and completely aware that they are seeing a real entity. The creature is likely not going to be a one-time sighting. It has been seen flying overhead, and it will follow the victim outside the home too. Even in the daylight, the creature has invaded the normal course of the day. It follows overhead, and casts a huge shadow when seen during broad daylight. No matter what the lighting or timing of the encounter, it always leaves its victim terrified and with a deep, permeating feeling of doom.

Amy M. Bruno
New Milford, Connecticut, 2015

This document is to serve as my, Amy M. Bruno, personal encounters with an unknown entity.

My first "sighting" of this entity was about five years ago. I was walking up my street at night. I got to a certain spot, which is where the creature has since always followed me from. This entity appears above me from behind, but "it" shows me what it looks like from a third-person view. The entity also has the power to interfere with my opinion of its behavior. I logically say, "This is not happening for real," but I cannot ignore the presence, the feeling, and the sight of the shadow creature. It appears as darker than the blackness of night, a winged "bat/human" creature.

In the beginning, it had no agenda with me. It just harmlessly flew above me as I turned around to go back home because of my fear of seeing it. The wings moved like a light curtain in the breeze. They never flapped. They were usually folded up otherwise.

186

I do believe it knows how I feel and what I was thinking when I encountered it. Over time, my fear grew with every appearance. The shadow creature preyed on that. To this day, I must estimate that I have had fifteen to twenty encounters, lasting from ten to forty-five minutes. In the more recent occurrences, it has escalated to going after the people I care for. At first, I was the only one to see the creature, but now it has visited my family, and they have seen it too.

When these visitations happen, the creature appears to become more detailed and clearer to me, as if I see it in more vivid detail. It looks more and more malevolent. The shadow creature chatters its numerous pointy sharp teeth or sits in a corner with its back toward you. The creature appears as if engineered to instill fear, and it knows that I perceive its teeth as most fearful of all sights associated with the creature. It reminded me of the teeth on Stephen King's *It*. The entity has also appeared incognito once.

Black-winged shadow creature. *Ilustration by Mike Mendes.*

The shadow was dressed in formal wear, with a top hat and tails on his tuxedo coat. It did nothing but stare at me. Its clothes stood still during its movement. This is the only instance that the creature caused something to make a noise. The floor beneath it creaked! The elegantly dressed nightmare then stood there for about a good five minutes, then walked away.

The Top Hat Man as described by Amy.
Illustration by Mike Mendes.

Another encounter was the most out of character for the thing, but I still knew that it was the same creature. I saw the black-winged shadow entity hover over my friend while she was sleeping. The entity enjoys taunting me. In addition to chattering its teeth, it shivers in a menacing way. There is no odor or other noticeable environmental changes with the phenomenon.

This thing appears to feed off my ultimate fears, and go after those I care for most. It is also fearful of light, any light. I kept the TV on at night to keep it at bay. When it appears and the TV is on, the entity remains at my bedroom entrance and stares at me. Other times it stays outside my window looking in, hovering and staring.

Why is this happening? I honestly have no idea, even though people I respect say it is feeding off of my sensitivity/weakness. I have tried to keep track of how I am feeling before and after these encounters. I did feel depressed, but it's difficult to know how much to credit the negative entity for that. I was also told that living by water can make these encounters more frequent. I do live near water and on Indian burial ground from the war.

Bill Hall Investigates, 2015

I told Amy to ignore it. Do not talk to it and do not think about it. As Shane prescribes,

> Erase it from her internal dialogue. It's going to be hard for her because she has been a victim her whole life to various scenarios. That is what she knows. It's time to stop being a victim physically and definitely stop being a victim of her thoughts. It is there because of the emotional frequency she is broadcasting. It will follow her. The entity most likely has nothing to do with her home. It's all about her. We must change her frequency.

These shadow creatures will drain the life out of you, like the vampires of lore. They are one of the biggest parasites out there, although some are quite positive. Shane has encountered guardian shadows as well. The negative type will do serious harm to your health.

The bottom line is: We needed to purge with positive and change her internal dialogue. Guilt is the most common baggage that we need to unload. She needs to let the bad memories go and live each day as a new life. Go forward. Do not live in the past.

Amy's Case Document Continued

Bill and I got together, and he explained how to get rid of these "parasites," as he called them. No religion, no sage, no protection spells, no nothing. In fact, he said nothing is the key. The power will come from you, he told me.

I started right away as prescribed. I kept thinking positive thoughts, reliving happy memories, and removing myself from my current location as often as possible. It worked just as promised.

Although I thanked Bill for getting rid of this thing, he reminded me that I did it. I told the creature that I am not afraid of it, and just like Bill and Shane said, it ran away scared. They warned me that because I cannot get out of the situation that fuels these negative thoughts, I need to work harder to build those skills, so a parasite cannot feed on that fear. It's empowering when you discover that these negative entities are not demons. There are no demons. These are entities, and they are not in control. You are. It's time to throw out sage and mysticism and what they do in horror movies. Instead, talk to Bill and his folks.

Case 3

When Trolls Attack

They're nasty, mean, and without any redeeming characteristics whatsoever. They seem happiest when they are terrorizing humans— stealing their cattle, imprisoning their children...
—Steve Benson

According to Scandinavian mythology, there are many types of trolls, and they are all very real. They can have a single head or multiple heads. They can be quite large, or quite small, with disproportionately smaller features, such as short stubby arms and legs, and often a fat belly. Some believe trolls are remnants of memories of Neanderthal humans. Certain types are believed to dwell in underground dark, damp caves, and Thor was known to kill them with his hammer (which might be why most people have never seen one).

Trolls are said to hate church bells and prefer to eat Christians as a result, although if they are famished, they will eat anyone (yes, like all the scariest legends, we're on the menu!). The good news is that, for at least the large version of the species, they turn to stone in the sunlight. And that's how the many large boulders ended up in Norway, so the story goes.

Although trolls are described as wrinkly and quite ugly to behold, mythology also bestows upon them the ability to shapeshift into whatever form they want to trick and enslave humans. Other times, they just want takeout.

Similar to UFO lore, trolls can keep you under their spell, and upon release, you will not remember the captivity. Instead, you will experience missing time. These creatures are also named to represent a variety of paranormal entities, including orcs, ogres, and other folklore monsters that secretly live out of sight, until they stumble during their missions.

Of all the variations of trolls that you might be unfortunate enough to encounter, the most dangerous and horrific is that of the trolls seen as three heads, or a group of three appearing as one. Our witnesses to these strange meetings saw these very creatures at their window.

Stacy
Bridgeport, Connecticut

Stacy is a personal friend of Bill Hall, who can vouch for her honesty and sanity.

Growing up, Stacy and her family lived in a three-family home in the top apartment. Stacey and her brother had their bedrooms on the attic floor of the apartment. There was a big chimney in the middle of the attic, then their two bedrooms were to the back.

One night, Stacy woke up startled at the sound of something scratching. "I thought it was a mouse, so I got scared. I look all around in an attempt to catch a glimpse of the perpetrator, but I was unsuccessful in finding anything," she explained.

She went back to bed and once again heard the scratching sounds.

"Behind the chimney, I finally saw it. I was looking straight at them. Three little ugly, ugly-looking trolls—that's how I would describe them, trolls," thinking out loud.

There was one on the bottom, another one on top of that one, and a third on top of that one! I swear to God—I freaked out! The faces were ugly! They had wrinkly faces and they were little. I don't remember noses, ears, or eyes. One arm reached around hugging the chimney, while their three disgusting faces peeked around as their heads bobbed about. I was so scared; the puzzle pieces came together as I realized the scratching came from them! Were they scratching at the window? Were they trying to get in the house? I ran back to my room.

The house where Stacy saw the trolls. *Photo by Bill Hall.*

Stacey went under the covers. She told us no more going by the chimney, even though you had to go past that to go downstairs. We asked questions about the scene, such as the lighting. Stacey says it was dark, but she had a little light in her bedroom.

She made it clear that there was no question as to what was seen. "It was no animal or owl. No way. I saw them clearly; they were like trolls."

Stacy never told anyone about this experience. She knew how crazy it sounded. And it was crazy. A few years later, she talked to her brother about that house and their attic bedrooms.

I asked my brother, "Matt, have you ever seen anything up there?"

Matt replied instantly, "Why, Stacy? You've seen them too?"

"Seen what?" Stacy asked.

"Those ugly little goblins or trolls. There were three of them, one on top of the other. They all looked the same."

Stacy's encounter was now confirmed. Matt saw them too. The same little wrinkly creatures peering into the attic hallway from the window while holding onto the exposed chimney. Stacy's mother told them when her brother was up there, he used to have skulls and light candles. Matt, however, said she is a bit old-fashioned and thought it was witchcraft, but they were only cool decorations.

Stacy turned to us and said, "To this day, whenever we talk about it, we both shake our heads. It was the weirdest thing, and only the two of us have seen it because we were the only two that lived up there."

Susan (Stacy's Mother) and Rosanne (Susan's Sister) Bridgeport, Connecticut

Bill Hall can vouch for Susan and Rosanne's honesty and sanity as well. This was not the first time that troll-like creatures invaded this family. The first encounters were many years before and significantly more sinister. This is their story.

I was six or seven years old and Rosanne was four or five years old when this happened. My parents owned a colonial house. Their bedroom was downstairs on the first floor and the upstairs attic level was made into bedrooms with a hallway between them. In order to get to the attic, we would have to go up wood stairs to the attic floor. At the top of the stairs on the right-hand side were four short doors that led to the eaves of the attic. The area was used for storage. The lighting up there was dim, just enough to navigate your way around.

One night, when reaching the top of the stairs, I looked to my right where the eave doors were, and I saw a creature slowly open one of the doors and peek its head out! It was a little wrinkly creature of some sort! In back of him, I saw more of those things.

Bill asked if I could make out their clothes or ears or any other details, but I couldn't. I can only tell you what I know I saw for sure. I was shivering in fear. These little folks were not good looking at all! I ran downstairs as soon as my legs would move again. Then I ran to tell my parents about the creatures in the crawlspace. Mom and Dad were not impressed. Naturally, they didn't believe me. Both responded by telling me to go back upstairs

A troll residence? *Photo by Bill Hall.*

and get to bed. I continued to see them many times. They would open one of the doors and peek out at me. More, no telling how many, were always behind the one that decided to peek out. The others would peer out too after stopping whatever it was they were doing.

I never spoke about these creatures to anyone until a get-together years later. My sister and I were both married and relaxing together with our husbands chatting. We were telling stories. I told my story about these little ugly, wrinkly people, and then Rosanne shocked me with her encounter, which was much more terrifying than mine—if that's even possible.

195

Trolls peeking out of an attic eave door. *Illustration by Mike Mendes.*

Rosanne was sleeping under the covers, and a few of these ugly creatures grabbed her legs and arms and started to pull her! They pulled and pulled until she was off the bed and on the floor beside her bed. Then they started to pull her again toward the doors that lead to the attic eaves. She kicked and swung her arms about as a natural reaction in an attempt to stop them from being able to drag her further.

The trolls were headed for the doors and trying to capture her! After struggling with all her might, she shook them loose. The creatures scuttled about as they rushed back to behind the crawlspace doors. Rosanne didn't mention it to anyone. She actually thought she must have been dreaming, although it was very real to her. She felt it. She felt where the wrinkly things grabbed her, she felt hitting the floor from the bed, but it is still caused her young mind to be baffled by the event. Therefore, it might be a dream. This would not be the creatures' last attempt.

An illustrated interpretation of trolls dragging Rosanne off her bed. *Illustration by Koren Harpaz.*

Some nights passed uneventfully and then it happened. Rosanne woke instantly to hands grabbing her arms and legs once again. She started struggling as the ugly assailants dragged her out of bed again for another fall onto the floor. Rosanne tried to scream for help, but she was so frightened that no sound came out of her when she tried. She struggled hard once again and won, as she escaped free from their clutches. Tiny little people scurried again for their crawlspace hideout. These attempts happened three or four times, Rosanne recalls.

Years later, the family moved to a three-family house that Susan's grandparents owned. This time, they were on the second floor. Both felt safer to be away from those unknown little weirdos. Until one night when Rosanne woke again to see several of them opening the closet door and running to her. They trapped her arms and legs tightly in their grasp as they tried to finally fulfill their mission. She was dragged from bed once again. They moved too! This time they were winning. Rosanne could not break free. The critters had pulled her all the way to right in front of the closet door. She gave everything she had as she realized this was her final chance to break free or else she would end up in the closet. Who knows what they wanted her for? The things were inside the closet and dragging Rosanne in. Finally, the moment came. She broke free, and their arms retreated into the closet as they quickly retreated and shut the closet door.

Both Susan and Rosanne remember them so vividly. It was a complete surprise. Susan told us,

> It really scared me when she told me about it. She never said anything about that to me. And it was not just one troll attacking her, there were at least a few of them. We both distinctly remember how quiet they were. They didn't make any noise, even when opening and closing the doors where they came from. Those little ugly wrinkly creatures were in there busy doing something, but I don't know what. I was too scared to ever investigate or go anywhere near those doors. I never will forget this. My sister and I will never forget it. Just when you thought they were gone and not going to come back, I would see them again.

Susan and Rosanne stressed that these were "real physical little beings." Jimmy and Bill are happy that the creatures were unsuccessful, especially if they follow trolls of lore and wanted a dinner and not a dinner guest. We wonder: Do these creatures follow generations, as in UFO encounters?

CASE 4

THE CURIOUS CASE OF THE MISSING MUFFINS

*The oldest and strongest emotion of mankind is fear, and the oldest
and strongest kind of fear is fear of the unknown.*
—H. P. Lovecraft

Investigated by Jimmy Petonito and Rick Clark

At around 7 p.m. on the evening of August 19, 1995, my phone rang. Fellow paranormal investigator Rick Clark also received the same call. The familiar voice of Lorraine Warren was on the other end. She and Ed were the founders of the New England Society for Psychic Research, and she needed our help.

Lorraine asked if we could check out a house in Waterbury, Connecticut. A terrified woman called and said she refused to go back into the house until someone came to help.

Off we went. Rick and I arrived about 8:30 p.m. Upon our arrival, we saw a young woman sitting on the front steps of a three-family home crying uncontrollably.

Melissa, relieved to see us, explained: "I keep seeing a shadow figure in my third-floor apartment. I don't want to go back inside!"

Together, we headed up the stairs to the third floor. Melissa turned the door knob back and forth, but the door would not open. She told us the door was not locked and there should be no reason why we couldn't get in. We all tried to move the knob and it moved freely. It wasn't locked, the knob turns, yet it wouldn't open. Next, Rick put his shoulder into the door like you see on TV and pushed. We all heard a big bang.

In front of the door, an exercise bicycle was tipped over. Melissa explained that the bike is kept on the other side of the room, and that's where it was when she left. The bike should have been in a spot some twelve feet away. Rick and I examined the back of the door. Strangely, it was locked. Melissa previously said she didn't have the key with her.

Our goal was to rule out whether she could have propped the bike under the door handle and went through the back door, leaving the door all set up for us. Further intrigued, we discovered that somehow the bicycle wedged itself on an angle underneath the doorknob in such a way that when we pushed the door open, it would fall and crash to the floor.

She voiced her fear since her twenty-six-year-old boyfriend, Scott, and her four-year-old son, Max, were away at the time. She was alone with whatever—or whoever—was in the apartment. We took a quick look in all the rooms to familiarize ourselves with the layout of the house. Then we settled in at the dining room table with Melissa to record her story.

They called this third-floor apartment home for almost a year. However, shortly after moving in, weird things began to happen. The couple never experienced any paranormal activity in any other residence.

Melissa had many complaints. She saw a shadow person on multiple occasions in different rooms at different times. Often, she is the only person who can see it.

Max told his mom, "I have a new friend. His name is Bobby and he's eight years old." This new "friend" would play with him. "It" was also mean to him. No one ever saw "Bobby" besides him. Also, Max often woke up with scratches and bruises. When his mom asked Max how he got them he said, "Bobby did it. Sometimes Bobby is mean."

Naturally, Melissa worried about what Max might be seeing, so she checked on him frequently. Their hallway was connected to the parent's bedroom and to the child's bedroom with a bathroom in between.

One evening, it was unusually quiet. Too quiet. Melissa slowly walked down the hallway to Max's room to see if she could catch what was going on. She walked toward the bedroom and froze in place, stunned by what she saw. Every toy in his room was piled on top of Max. He was sound asleep.

Trying to not startle and wake him, she began removing the toys from the bed. They were stacked in such a way that it looked impossible for him to do it himself. They would all fall over if you tried to set up a pile of toys that way yourself. Max woke up to toys being removed from on top of him. Melissa asked him what happened. He said Bobby did it.

When Melissa made any kind of treats, like muffins or cookies, she put them on a dish and stored them on top of the refrigerator toward the back. This way, Max wouldn't notice the treats and eat them. Melissa relayed to us two incidents of missing muffins and cookies. They vanished and reappeared in another place.

One morning, while Max was in preschool, she made a dozen muffins. Following the usual routine, she put them on a plate, set them on top of the refrigerator, and slid them to the back. When they returned to the house in the afternoon, the muffins were gone. The plate was still there. She asked Scott if he knew anything about it, but he never even knew that muffins were made. Later that week when Melissa was cleaning out Max's closet, she found all the muffins stacked in the left corner.

Another time, she baked chocolate chip cookies, wrapped them up on a plate, and put them in the usual hiding place. They disappeared altogether. One evening, they had a few friends over to visit. They sat at the kitchen table and enjoyed lively conversation. From the kitchen, you can see slightly into the living room/dining room combination. On the opposite side of the kitchen, you can see into the hallway and the bathroom door.

Melissa looked up and noticed her son standing near the couch, which is right around the corner in the living room. He looked confused and focused. He was pointing behind the couch. She got up to see what he was pointing at; it was the missing cookies. The whole batch was stacked up behind the couch!

Since Melissa's boyfriend works long hours at night, Kim's mom suggested that she go over to Melissa's. She welcomed the help with Max, and especially loved having someone else there. It had become simply too scary to stay there alone.

Kim's mom, Jackie, was the niece of Gerard Godin of the Bridgeport Poltergeist case, the subject of Bill Hall's unprecedented work *The World's Most Haunted House: The True Story of the Bridgeport Poltergeist on Lindley Street* (subtle plug).

Rick and I interviewed Kim and asked if she ever witnessed anything odd. She told us, "The little boy had LA Gear sneakers, you know, the ones with lights in the heel. With motion pressure or movement, it makes the lights blink red. Every so often, the sneakers blinked at me. It felt as if those sneakers were mocking me."

I asked, "What makes you think that?"

She continued, "The sneakers were blinking, I turned my head to look at them, and then they'd stop. That's usually how it always happened."

Then she became silent for a moment before telling us, "I was walking down the hallway to Max's room. I can see the sneakers in plain view. They didn't just move. The sneakers took three steps! They actually 'walked' by themselves. It was unreal!"

Rick and I decided to test the sneakers. If you push on the heel, they will blink. If you shake them really hard, they will blink. And if you stomp your feet right next to them, they will also blink. They would *not* blink just by someone simply walking around close to them.

This all happened before the internet. I did some old-fashioned detective work and called Bob's Stores to get the phone number for LA Gear. I told them about the unprovoked blinking and asked if this kind of thing can happen. They had no explanation. "No way could this happen," the stern voice said. Well, that was an awkward call.

For the duration of the interview, Melissa kept pointing in different directions to a "figure" that remained unseen to us.

"There it is! Don't you see it? There it is!" She excitedly pointed out.

No. We're sorry. We don't.

She narrates its action: "It just walked into my bedroom!" Curious, we ask her what it looked like.

"It's like a shadow, a shadow of a person against a wall, but in the middle of the room," she tried to explain.

We decided to relocate to the living room to see if we could see the figure. The stupidest move of the night was not bringing our cameras with us. We didn't expect to see anything.

From the living room, we finally saw it. The shadow was standing in the left corner of her bedroom about two feet from the left wall and about two feet from the back wall.

Her description was accurate. It was a shadow—a shadow standing in the middle of the room. The male figure was dark grey in color, slim, and about five feet, ten inches tall. Rick and I just looked at each other. I told Rick about my dilemma. I wanted to get my video camera in the other room, but I was worried it might be gone when I come back. I also wanted to witness what it might do.

Rick turned to me and settled it. "Let's go up to it and touch it."

The shadow male was about seven feet away from us. We took a few steps toward it. As we slowly walked toward it, the creature turned to the right, took one small step, and disappeared by melting into the left wall. We walked around the wall to see if it appeared on the other side. There was nothing.

The remainder of the evening was uneventful. We returned the next evening to recreate the cookies on the refrigerator "scene." This time, we aimed our video camera at the proper area of the fridge with hopes of capturing our elusive mischief maker. Hours passed. Nothing.

Melissa had an incident while in the shower. No one else was home. The lights began to blink in the bathroom. The shower curtain was pushed violently to the side, and she saw the shadow person! She screamed, grabbed a towel, and ran out of the bathroom and then out of the house with just with her towel on.

The part of the wall where the shadow passed. *Photo courtesy of Rick Clark.*

Rick and I returned in late August. The couple moved out. Their lease was up at the end of the month, and they weren't going to chance it anymore. The only items left in the house were a small white night table and—you guessed it—those haunted blinking sneakers.

I asked, "Why aren't you taking the sneakers?"

Melissa answered, "Would you want sneakers that looked at you and walked by themselves?" I didn't say yes. Nevertheless, I have "sole" custody of them.

The couple told us we were free to do any kind of experiments; basically, anything we wanted to do in the apartment. Now without power, the apartment was getting dark. The only light was our one flashlight.

We started our experiment. I placed the sneakers on top of the small night table, found a small Matchbox car, and put that on the table too. The video camera joined the other objects on the table. We diligently watched the setup with hope the car would fly off the table and that the sneakers would move or at least blink. Nothing happened.

I had a thought. A lot of the activity happens when no one is home, especially the cookies and muffins. Out loud I said, "Perhaps the sneakers suffer from stage fright? Okay, we're going to go downstairs."

We head down three flights of stairs to the outside and sit on the stairs talking for about twenty minutes. After returning, we we're disappointed to see that nothing had changed.

The actual sneakers during testing. Jimmy have "saved these soles" for many years. *Photo by Jimmy Petonito.*

The video set up with the sneakers. *Photo by Jimmy Petonito.*

In the now dark house, we decide to check the other rooms using the flashlight as our limited guide. Melissa and I were talking close by in the hallway near the bathroom.

Suddenly, I heard a male voice right in my ear: "Hey. Hey you!"

Right then, Melissa says, "Did you hear that? I heard a man's voice say 'Hey. Hey you!'"

I'm not sure why, but hearing a disembodied voice talk in my ear was scarier than seeing the shadow figure!

Back to Max's room, we checked on the camera to see if it caught the sneakers do their thing. I rewound the tape to the part when I announced that we were leaving. Press play. You can hear us say we're leaving. You hear the door close. Moments later, a sneaker starts blinking! First the right one, then the left one. Then they blink in unison. Then they blink back and forth. There was no one walking, no loud booms, and no other movement. Nothing.

I thought to try to use the sneakers as a communication device. "Blink once if you're a male and twice if you're a female," I instructed.

The left speaker blinked red once. This is all on a creepier level now because it's almost dark, the room is almost all gray, and you could just barely make out the sneakers. When they blinked, their lights were bright and powerful.

Next, I asked for age. By counting with pauses in between to give time to respond, I started: 1, 2, 3, 4, 5, 6, 7, 8. My counting was interrupted by a clear answer. The sneakers started blinking rapidly, almost as if excited to share the information with us.

Jimmy revisits the missing muffin house. *Photo by Bill Hall.*

THE CURIOUS CASE OF THE MISSING MUFFINS

The small family officially moved completely out the next day while I snapped a photo of the truck pulling away.

The sneakers? I took the sneakers home and put them on the TV. Although it was only the beginning of September, I already decorated early for Halloween as always. (Our apartment was full of decorations. We had a mat outside our door that would scream when you stepped on it. There were four witches and goblins that hung from the ceiling that would shudder and shake and yell "Happy Halloween!" when you clapped.)

On this particular evening, we were headed out to an overnight investigation. My wife was home watching TV on one of those old wooden console TVs. She didn't know what happened last night because we didn't get the chance to catch up.

While watching a scary movie, her eyes catch the little sneakers on top of the TV. Our report of the night's incidents were underneath the sneakers. She grabs the report and returns to the couch to read it. Then she gets to the part about the sneakers. She's looking up at the sneakers and back at the report. At the same time, the outdoor mat screams, all of the four-foot decorations shook and said "Happy Halloween!" while the sneakers proudly started blinking.

Arriving home at 5 a.m., I am greeted at my front door by two little LA Gear sneakers. Someone put them outside. I head inside to find my wife nervous and tired. She didn't sleep all night. She looked up at me shaking her head. "Never again! Never again! You know I didn't listen."

A mutual friend that lived on the second floor of the apartment in Waterbury updated us that new tenants moved in. Already, the tenant complained that his cigarettes he keeps in the refrigerator keep vanishing. I advised her to have him check the closets and behind the couch.

BIBLIOGRAPHY

Andrews, Colin, and Synthia Andrews. *On the Edge of Reality: Hidden Technology, Powers of the Mind, Quantum Physics, Paranormal Phenomena, Orbs, UFOs, Harmonic Transmissions, and Crop Circles.* New Page Books, 2013.

"Are Friends Electric." *Fortean Times.* FT108, March 1998, page 40.

Bernard, Dennis. *Meadow Cottage—Things that Go Bump in the Night! Local Life,* Summer 2015.

Borra, E.F., and E. Trottier. "Discovery of Peculiar Periodic Spectral Modulations in a Small Fraction of Solar Type Stars," Département de Physique, Université Laval, Québec, QC G1V 0A6, Canada, published 14 October 2016.

Cardoso, Anabela. *Electronic Contact with the Dead: What Do the Voices Tell Us?* White Crow Books, 2017.

Cooper, Callum E. *Telephone Calls from the Dead.* Tricorn Books, 2012.

"Emails from the Dead—The Jack Froese Story." *Historicmysteries.com,* 11 April 2016.

Floyd, E. Randall. *In the Realm of Ghosts and Hauntings*. Harbor House, 2002.

Fowler, Raymond E., and J. Allen Hynek. *The Andreasson Affair: The True Story of a Close Encounter of the Fourth Kind*. New Page Books, 2014.

"Ghost Stories: Visits from the Deceased," *Scientific American*, 2 December 2008.

Hallowell, Michael J. *The South Shields Poltergeist*. History Press Ltd, UK edition, 2009.

Harari, Yuval Noah. *Homo Deus: A Brief History of Tomorrow*. Harper, 2017.

Houdini, Harry. *A Magician Among the Spirits*. Harper and Brothers, 1924.

Hopkins, Budd. *Intruders: The Incredible Visitations at Copley Woods*. Random House, 1987.

Locher, Theo. *Swiss Bulletin for Parapsychology*. November 1986.

"Man Believes Dead Wife Is Contacting Him on Mobile," *Blackpool Gazette*, 27 March 2008.

"Metrolink Collision: NTSB Tries to Sort It All Out," *Los Angeles Times*, 17 September 2008.

Paton, James. *The Black Book of Ghosts, UFO's and the Unexplained*. James Paton, 2013.

Ramsland, Katherine. *Dean Koontz: A Writer's Biography*. Harper Prism, 1998.

Redfern, Nick. *The Real Men in Black: Evidence, Famous Cases, and True Stories of These Mysterious Men and Their Connection to UFO Phenomena*. New Page Books, 2011.

Redfern, Nick. *Women in Black: The Creepy Companions of the Mysterious M.I.B. Paperback*. Lisa Hagen Books, 2016.

Ridsdel, Wayne, and Cyrilla Crow. *Poltergeist Then and Now*. Wayne Ridsdel and Cyrilla Crow, 3 September 2013.

Rogo, D. Scott, and Raymond Bayless. *Phone Calls from the Dead: The Results of a Two-Year Investigation into an Incredible Phenomenon.* Prentice Hall, 1979.

Sarfatti, Jack. *Destiny Matrix.* AuthorHouse, 2002.

Vasey, G. Michael. *Ghost in the Machines: Scary True Stories of the Paranormal: How Ghosts and Demons Hijack Technology (True Paranormal Stories Book 4).* Asteroth's Books, 2015.

Webster, Ken. *The Vertical Plane.* Grafton, 1989.

"What May Happen in the Next Hundred Years," *Ladies' Home Journal,* December 1900.

About the Authors

WILLIAM J. HALL, author of the paranormal bestseller *The World's Most Haunted House: The True Story of the Bridgeport Poltergeist on Lindley Street* and *The Haunted House Diaries* returns to explore another paranormal phenomenon. Hall is professionally equipped to recognize trickery: After more than twenty-five years as a performing magician, he knows how to create and recognize illusions. He is also an experienced researcher of the unexplained, from folklore and urban legend to fortune-telling, the pyramids, and other mysterious tales. Bill has been interviewed around the world and his syndicated column, Magic and the Unknown, ran for six years in multiple newspapers. Hall has two sons and resides in Plainville, Connecticut.

JIMMY PETONITO began investigating with Ed and Lorraine Warren and has gone on to explore the unknown for more than thirty years. He has appeared on numerous television shows such as *Sightings, Unsolved Mysteries, Primetime Live,* and *Hostage to the Devil* (documentary), and his cases have been featured on shows such as Canada's *Scariest Night of My Life* and others. Jimmy is also the host of the popular radio program *The Haunted Chronicles*. He is often called "Mr. Haunted." Petonito resides with his wife and two beautiful daughters, Heidi and Holly, in Cheshire, Connecticut.

More from Jimmy Petonito and William J. Hall

Gift Shop, Contact, Aid in Active Hauntings
halloftheparanormal.com
or
mrhaunted.com

Speaking Engagements

Jimmy and Bill are available for speaking engagements for your organization, club, or group. A powerful and fun presentation followed by Q&A and a book signing.

Bulk Sales for Your Group or Fundraiser

If you are interested in bulk sales for your group, book club, paranormal society, or fundraiser, we can put together a package just for you!

The Haunted Chronicles: Jimmy Petonito's Radio Show

Listen in and participate to this popular paranormal radio show with your host Jimmy! Visit *mrhaunted.com* for more information.

If You Enjoyed this Book

Please review it online at *amazon.com* or *barnesandnoble.com*. Check out these other titles by William J. Hall:

The Worlds Most Haunted House:
The True Story of the Bridgeport Poltergeist on Lindley Street

The Haunted House Diaries: The True Story of a Quiet Connecticut
Town in the Center of a Paranormal Mystery

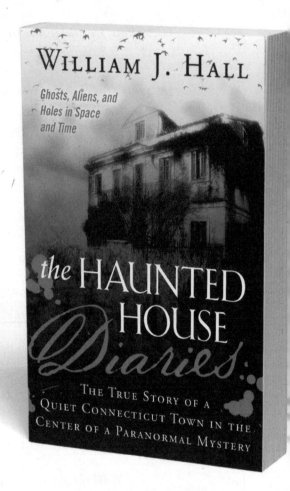

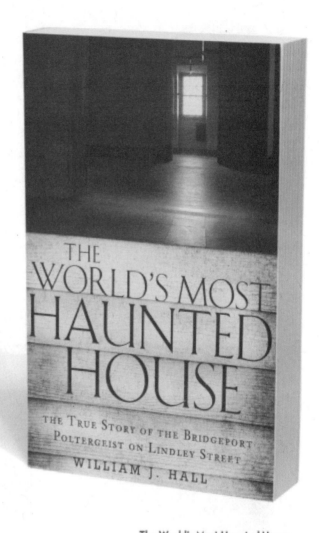

ALSO FROM NEW PAGE BOOKS

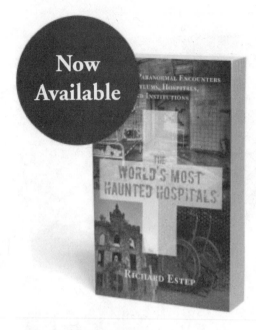